Disaster with the Fiend

Collins
RED
STORYBOOK

...na Lavelle

Holiday with the Fiend

Other Collins Red Storybooks

SHEILA LAVELLE

Disaster with
the Fiend

Illustrated by
Margaret Chamberlain

CollinsChildren'sBooks
An Imprint of HarperCollinsPublishers

First published in Great Britain by
Hamish Hamilton Children's Books 1988
First published by Collins 1991

3 5 7 9 10 8 6 4 2

Collins is an imprint of
HarperCollins*Publishers* Ltd,
77-85 Fulham Palace Road,
Hammersmith, London W6 8JB.

Text copyright © 1988 by Sheila Lavelle
Illustrations copyright © 1988 by Margaret Chamberlain

ISBN 0 00 673669-6

The author and illustrator assert the moral right to be
identified as the author and illustrator of the work.

Printed and bound by Caledonian International
Book Manufacturing, Scotland

To Nicola Worbey, Jessica Davis,
and Dwight Scholes
with love and thanks

Chapter One

I knew Angela's birthday party was going to be really special. She has always had fabulous parties, ever since her dad built that enormous extra room for her on top of their garage and there's enough space to invite the whole class. And because her birthday is only a couple of weeks before Christmas, they put all the decorations up and the room looks great. You don't have to sit around eating fish-paste sandwiches and playing stupid card-games or Consequences like you do at other people's parties, either. Oh, no. Nothing boring like that.

At Angela's parties they get caterers in. There's things like smoked salmon and chicken legs and sausages on sticks and delicious little sandwiches stuffed with asparagus and liver pâté and big bowls of yummy cheesy stuff to dip your crisps and lumps of celery in and my favourite chocolate gateau and that lemon cheesecake that melts in your mouth like snowflakes. And instead of kids' party games they bring in the cassette player and you dance to loud music that shakes the street. And Angela's mum makes big jugs of her special non-alcoholic punch which tastes just as good as the stuff they served at my cousin Fiona's wedding and maybe even better.

So I was really looking forward to Angela's birthday, until a few days before the party that is, when she showed me the new dress she was planning to wear. That spoiled everything, I can tell you, because I knew I only had my awful old green tartan thing with the white collar and horrible plastic belt that I'd worn to Angela's last party, as well as every other party I had been to for the past twelve months. Why is it that mums can afford new dresses for themselves every five minutes, with shoes and handbags and hairdos and everything else to match, while they moan like mad if you ask for even a new pair of school socks?

Anyway, there I was lying on my bed with my dog Daniel, giggling over a comic and wiping my eyes on the corner of the bedspread, when who should come charging up the stairs and into my bedroom without so much as a knock at the door but Angela. Her face was as pink as toilet-paper with excitement and those big blue eyes of hers were sparkling like fairy lights, the way they always do when she's especially pleased with herself.

"Move over, Daniel," she said, shoving him off the bed. "Here, Charlie. Just have a look at this." She dumped a big, flat, white box on the bedspread and started taking off the lid.

I slid off the bed and stood beside her, and I knew from the *Arabella* label that it was going to be something out of the ordinary. Angela rustled among the layers of tissue paper and then drew out the most fabulous party dress I had ever seen.

"How about that," she said, gloating like the cat that got the caviare. "It cost forty-five pounds ninety-five at *Arabella's*. Wait until you see me in it."

She went to my dressing table mirror and held the dress against her, and I could see she would look great in it. It was made of shiny satin, the same blue as her eyes, the sleeves were huge batwing shapes with gathered cuffs, and the pleated skirt was so short it was practically non-existent.

"What do you think, Charlie?" she said, turning round. "Isn't it brill?"

"Everybody will see your knickers when you bend down," I said sourly. For the life of me I couldn't say anything nice.

Angela burst out laughing. "So what?" she said. "It's all the fashion these days. Anyway, look. Knickers and tights to match, so it doesn't matter." She delved once more into the box and came up with the tights and satin knickers of the exact same shade of blue. "I've got new shoes as well, of course," she boasted, twirling about so that the dress floated around her.

"Of course," I said. "Naturally." But she didn't seem to notice my bad mood. She laid the dress tenderly back among its tissues and then opened my wardrobe door.

"What are you going to wear, Charlie?" she said, rummaging about among my clothes as if it was a jumble sale. "Not that frumpy old tartan thing again, I hope? It's like something out of the dustbin."

I sat down on my bed and leaned casually back against the pillows. "As a matter of fact," I said airily, "I'm having a new dress, too. My mum's taking me to Barlow tomorrow." I pushed Angela's box away from me with my foot as if there was a bad smell coming out of it. "I expect we'll go to *Martine's*," I said. "*Arabella's* stuff always seems just a shade tacky, somehow."

With a scowl that would have stopped a charging elephant, Angela grabbed her box and made for the door.

"You're jealous, Charlotte Ellis," she shouted at me, sticking out her tongue. And, pleased with the sound of her rhyme, off she flounced, shouting, "Jealous, jealous, Charlie Ellis", all the way down the stairs, along the drive, and round the corner to her own house next door.

I rolled over and put my head under the pillow. Sometimes she makes me so mad I could scream. Having a friend like Angela Mitchell is like being friends with one of those poisonous snakes that wave about in baskets in India. You never know when she's going to strike next.

My dad says she's more of a *fiend* than a friend and what she really needs is a good kick up the backside. He says I should get myself another friend and tell Angela to jump in the fishpond, but it's not easy when somebody lives next door and your mums are best friends and go every-where together, even the ladies' loo. I've tried lots of times to get rid of her, but she keeps turning up and there's not really a lot I can do except try to get my own back now and again.

I was still lying there with my head under the pillow and Daniel was trying to dig me out, when my dad came to tell me that tea was ready and that it was fried chicken and chips and peas. He knew there was something really wrong with me when I said I didn't want any, because I've never refused fried chicken and chips and peas in my life before.

"Come on, Charlie, bonny lass," said my dad, pulling the pillow off my head. "Tell your old dad about it." And before I knew what was happening, I found myself spilling out the whole story about the party and not having a new dress and being ashamed of being seen in that old tartan rag that looked like something off the compost heap.

"I won't go to the rotten party," I sobbed, wiping my nose on my sleeve. "If I can't have something nice to wear, I'd rather not go at all."

My dad gave me his hanky, a screwed-up greyish thing that looked as if he'd been cleaning his shoes on it.

"Poor Cinderella," he said, smiling. "You get more like your mother every day. She never has anything to wear, either." He stood up and pulled me to my feet. "Come and get your tea, and I promise to see what I can do. OK?"

"OK," I said, my tears disappearing like magic, because when my dad promises something you can bet your boots that everything will turn out right.

And it did. The very next afternoon, straight after school, there I was in *Martine's Young Fashions* with my mum, trying on posh party dresses that I had never even dreamed of. My mum and dad had sat up quite late the night before, talking about me and my problems, and I had been dying to creep downstairs to listen at the door like I used to do when I was three. I didn't hear anything they said, but it didn't matter. All that mattered was that the next day my dad drew fifty pounds out of his savings account for my new dress, and when he told me about it I squeezed him so hard that his eyes almost fell out of his head.

"That's all right, Charlie," he grinned. "You're quite a grown-up young lady now, and your mum and I mustn't forget it."

Martine's dresses were so lovely I had a hard time choosing, and I could see my mum was getting a bit fed-up with hanging around.

"Come on, Charlie," she said impatiently. "There must be one you like. I think the blue one looked nicest." I didn't remind her of all the times I'd waited for hours while she'd tried on a few thousand hats or several hundred pairs of shoes.

"It's too much like Angela's," I said. "I don't want anything blue."

"What about this?" the spiky-haired salesgirl suddenly said, coming back with something over her arm. "It's not a dress, exactly. But it might do."

As soon as I saw it my heart turned over about six times and I knew that this was it. The colour wasn't exactly red, and it wasn't exactly orange, but it was a sort of glowing flame shade somewhere in between. And it wasn't a dress, it had three separate pieces. There was a tiny vest-like thing with narrow shoulder-straps, a full swirling skirt with big pockets, and a matching baggy jacket with long sleeves and cuffs with a hundred little buttons on. I loved it at once.

And when I tried it on I loved it even more. The colour suited my sun-tanned face and dark hair, and when I twirled about the shiny material glowed and shimmered in the shop lights.

"She looks wonderful in it," smirked the assistant, and I could see that my mum thought so, too. Then the bomb dropped. "It's a real bargain at sixty-three pounds," the girl went on, and my poor heart turned over one more time and sank to the bottom of my stomach like a dead kipper.

My mum looked at my face. She looked at the flame-coloured dress. She stared at the floor for a minute. I stared at the salesgirl's green spiky hair and she stared at her purple fingernails. Nobody said anything for a long time.

"We'll take it," my mum said at last, with a huge sigh, and I would have hugged her except I didn't want to get my new clothes all messed up before I'd had them less than five minutes.

"It'll be bread and jam for the rest of the month," grumbled my mum on the way home in the bus. "That extra money came out of the housekeeping."

I didn't care. I clutched the precious parcel to me as if it was an Olympic Gold Medal, and all I could think about was Angela's face when she saw it. It would make her groan with envy, and with any luck she'd never speak to me again. That would be the best thing of all.

She was waiting in the drive when we got

home, even though it was freezing cold and starting to snow. But I wouldn't show her my dress. "You'll see it on Saturday," was all I said. And I shut the door right in her face.

At school next day she did her best to wheedle it out of me, and I was so pleased with myself that I just couldn't help dropping hints about how gorgeous it was.

"Not nicer than mine, though, Charlie," she pleaded. "That wouldn't be very kind of you. It is my party, after all."

I took a deep breath. "It's ten times nicer than yours," I declared. "It makes yours look like a . . . a fishmonger's overall!"

Angela opened her mouth and closed it again. Then she walked off without a word.

I was walking home from school on the Friday afternoon, the day before the party, when Laurence Parker came puffing along behind.

"I've got something to tell you, Charlie," he told me, glancing furtively over his shoulder to see if anyone was listening. "That Angela Mitchell is going to try and make you look a right idiot, and it's not fair."

I stared at him. Although we're in the same

class, we've never been exactly the best of friends, and I couldn't understand what he was getting at.

"What do you mean," I demanded. "She can't make me look an idiot. I've got a lovely new dress for the party tomorrow, and she's jealous, that's all."

"That's just it," said Laurence hurriedly. "Listen, Charlie. She'll kill me if she finds out I've told you. She doesn't want anyone to give the secret away." He unwrapped a toffee from the never-ending supply in his pocket and stuffed it into his mouth.

"What secret?" I scowled, wondering what Angela could be up to now.

"She's deshided to have everybody in fanshy dresh," mumbled Laurence, chewing the toffee. "There's going to be a prize for the funniest costume. She's giving a ten-pound vulture."

"A what?" I gaped. "You mean a Christmas turkey or something?"

"Nah," he said irritably. "A vulture for ten quid. What you can spend in Boots or Smiths or somewhere like that."

I was too upset to laugh. "A voucher, you

mean, you great stupid twit," I said impatiently. "A ten-pound voucher, not a vulture. A vulture's a big squawky bird. It's huge and ugly and it never stops eating." Like you, I felt like adding, but I thought I'd better not. He might go off in a huff without telling me anything more.

"Well, anyway," said Laurence, his cheek bulging. "Everyone's coming as cartoon characters. All except you. You'll be the only one that's not in fancy dress, and you're meant to feel a proper fool." He stuffed his hands in his pockets and looked red and embarrassed. "But I think it's a rotten trick, so I decided to tell you. So you can get a fancy dress as well, see? Spoil her horrible plan."

I was so mad I couldn't speak. I stomped off home with my eyes full of tears and didn't even thank Laurence Parker for giving the game away. To think that Angela could be so mean and cruel to me when I was supposed to be her best friend. But that wasn't the worst thing. The worst thing was that I wouldn't be able to wear my wonderful dress after all, and we'd bought it all for nothing.

I cheered up a bit when I got home because my dad was back early, as he often is on a Friday. 'Poets' day', he calls it, which means 'Push Off Early, Tomorrow's Saturday', only he doesn't say push, he says something else which is too rude to repeat.

Anyway, he laughed like anything when I told him what Laurence had told me and said what a minx that Angela was but at least we had found out in time. And after our supper of steak and kidney pie and potatoes baked in their jackets, we got to work and made me the funniest fancy dress costume you ever saw.

It was a Minnie Mouse outfit, and we got the idea from a cartoon on the telly. It was dead easy to make because I already had a little black velvet hat that I could sew big, black felt ears onto, and black tights to which I could attach a long tail. I cut an old white dress very short and made a big, spotted bow for the neck, and my mum lent me some long spiky false eyelashes and a pair of high-heeled shoes with silver buckles that she must have worn in the Ark. And when I had got everything on and looked at myself in the mirror I laughed so much I was almost sick on the carpet and that would have been an awful waste of steak and kidney pie and jacket potato. Daniel took one look at me, then dived under the sofa and wouldn't come out.

"Your nose!" said my dad suddenly. "You must have a proper mouse nose." And he got a ping-pong ball and carefully cut a hole in it so that it fitted over my own nose. Then he painted it bright red, and it was the perfect finishing touch. "We'll see what Miss Cleverclogs Mitchell thinks of that!" snorted my dad, and I couldn't wait to find out.

Saturday came at last. The party was due to start at five o'clock, so at about four I wrapped up Angela's birthday present, a lovely pink cashmere scarf that had cost me two months' pockey money, and then spent about an hour getting dressed. My dad kept laughing so much he wasn't any help at all, but at five o'clock I was ready, complete with the red-painted nose.

I decided to go a bit late when everybody else had already arrived. My costume would have the most effect that way, and Angela would be all the more furious. I sat on the window seat in my room, thinking longingly of chocolate gateau. I tried to coax Daniel to let me stroke him, but he only growled at me and raised the hairs on the back of his neck. He didn't like the look of me at all.

At half-past five I tottered off in my high-heeled shoes down the cold slushy drive and round the corner to Angela's house. The windows above the garage were open a little and I could hear the music and people talking and laughing. Angela's mum came to the back door when I knocked, and she gave such a shriek when she saw me I thought she was going to faint.

"Good grief, Charlie! Is that really you?" she gasped. "What a fright you gave me." She stared at me slowly from head to foot, looking more and more uncomfortable by the second.

"It's a wonderful outfit, Charlie," she said. "But I think I ought to tell you . . ."

I was too impatient to listen. I knew I was sure to win first prize, and I was dying to see Angela's face.

"Tell me later, Auntie Sally," I begged. "I'm

late for the party already." And I hurried past her up the stairs.

I opened the door to Angela's playroom and my heart gave this awful lurch and then stopped beating altogether because the first thing I saw was Angela flaunting herself around in her *blue Arabella dress*. And as I looked around the room it hit me like a ton of horse-manure that all the kids were dressed in posh party clothes, with the boys in trendy designer jeans and smart ironed shirts and the girls in bright silk and satin dresses and pretty tights and patent leather shoes and *not one single person was wearing fancy dress*.

Just me. Stupid gullible old me. Me with my ridiculous red nose and my daft mouse ears and my long tail trailing on the ground. And one by one the other kids began to notice me and to point and shriek with laughter and what with the yelling and shouting and the shrieking and the music playing at full blast the noise was deafening.

Angela suddenly turned off the music and everybody went quiet.

"Oh, Charlie," she giggled. "You really fell

for it this time. Laurence must have been very convincing." She twirled herself around, showing off the satin skirt of her dress.

"Anyway, your costume looks great," she said. "What do you think of mine?"

I glared at her fiercely, wishing I was a witch so I could turn her into a toad.

"I've only got one thing to say to you, Angela Mitchell," I burst out at last. "Like I told you before, your bum shows when you bend down."

And I clattered away down the stairs, kicking holes in their posh wallpaper as I went, and telling myself exactly what she could do with her birthday parties in future, chocolate gateau or no chocolate gateau.

Chapter Two

ANGELA and I were waiting at the bus stop at the end of the road one cold windy morning in the Christmas holidays, sharing a bag of jelly babies and telling each other silly jokes. Angela was in one of her good moods for a change because we were going to Barlow to do some shopping, and spending money is what she likes best in the whole world.

"Which end of a jelly baby do you eat first, Charlie?" she asked me, fishing a red one

19

out of the bag and licking the icing sugar off it.

"I dunno," I said, stamping my feet to try to keep warm. "Its head, I suppose. I haven't really thought about it."

"I eat their feet first," said Angela gleefully, nipping off the jelly baby's pink toes with her sharp white teeth. "Then they can't run away!" And she gave an evil grin like a vampire about to drink a bucket of fresh blood.

"Oh, Angela. Don't be so horrible," I begged, putting my own jelly baby back in the bag. Somehow I didn't feel like eating any more, and I expect that's why she said it because she scoffed the whole lot herself in the bus on the way to Barlow.

We were going shopping for a wedding present for Angela's cousin, Felicity Frensham-Pond, who was getting married in two weeks' time. Both our families had been invited to the wedding, and to the reception at a big posh hotel in Beaconsmead. Our mums had already bought their presents, boring things like toasters and electric kettles, but Angela thought it would be nice if we girls gave something of our own.

I thought it was a rotten idea, actually. I get very little pocket money as it is, and spending it on a present for Felicity Frensham-Pond, who I've never even met, and who probably has a million times more money than me, seemed just plain stupid. But Angela persuaded me as usual, and as I know for a fact that she's never short of pocket money I consoled myself with the thought that maybe I wouldn't have to put very much towards it.

At least she behaved herself on the bus for once. Sometimes she does the most awful things and makes me ashamed to be with her – like the time the bus was full of old ladies going to the Post Office to get their pensions and she started pretending we were French girls over here on holiday.

"Thees bus? Eez going to Weendsor, no?" she said, leaning over and patting a grey-haired old lady on the arm.

"Pardon?" said the lady, looking at the person sitting next to her for help, "What did the child say? Weendsor?"

The other lady must have once been a schoolteacher because she immediately took over in a very bossy manner.

"She means Windsor, Nelly. You know, where the Queen lives. She thinks this bus is going to Windsor." She leaned over the first lady's lap and addressed Angela in the loud voice that English people always use with foreigners, as if they were deaf or stupid or both.

"You'd better get off at the next stop, dear," she shouted. "This bus is going to Barlow, I'm afraid. You'll have to get the number twenty-three."

Angela nodded and smiled. "Thees bus go to Barlow, yes? And then, after, he go to Weendsor, no?"

"NO!" said both old ladies together, and began to explain all over again.

Angela kept nodding and smiling and pretending she didn't understand until finally the bossy lady leaned forward and tapped the driver on the shoulder.

"Excuse me, driver," she said. "These young French girls think they are on the bus to Windsor. Perhaps you'd kindly stop and let them off."

The driver looked in his mirror and grinned when he saw that it was me and Angela.

"French girls, my eye," he said with a snort. "Those two live in Edgebourne. They've been on this bus dozens of times. They're having you on, lady."

And of course by now everybody in the bus was listening to what was going on and Angela couldn't help falling about giggling while they all tutted and muttered and asked each other what the world was coming to these days.

Today, however, the bus was almost empty, and Angela was as good as gold. We got off in Barlow and wandered down the High Street. We looked in the shop windows, still decorated in their tatty Christmas tinsel, and tried to think of brilliant ideas. It's not easy buying a present for somebody who's so rich they've got everything they want anyway, and we soon got fed-up and bored with the whole thing. Then we turned the corner at the bottom of the street and found the very shop.

It must have been newly-opened because we hadn't seen it before, and when we went inside there was every kind of present you could think of. Copper kettles and plant hangers and brass elephants and carved ivory statues and fringed shawls and woven baskets and cuckoo clocks and painted plates and old books and paintings and all kinds of stuff. It all looked sort of different, some antique stuff and some a bit foreign, and nothing like the sort of boring things that other shops in Barlow seem to sell.

We gazed around, and I could see that Angela was just as enchanted as me.

"Now, young ladies, can I help you?" said a voice suddenly, and a small man with bushy black hair and very squeaky shoes came through a bead curtain at the back of the shop. And he turned out to be extremely helpful, even if he did have thick curly bristles sticking out of his nostrils as if some small furry animal lived up his nose.

After we'd finished staring at his nose we explained about the wedding present, and in no time at all he suggested the ideal thing.

"I have a special ornamental plate," he said, rubbing his hairy hands together in the cold. "It has the bride and groom in wedding costume painted on it by hand. Would you like to see it?"

"Yes, please," said Angela, beaming. But I wasn't so sure.

"Er . . . how much is it?" I asked, feeling for the fifty-pence piece which was all I had in my pocket.

"Oh, very cheap," he replied. "Only five pounds fifty." And he went squeaking away through the bead curtain at the back.

I looked round for Angela to ask her if she had enough money, and found her fingering a pretty gold chain with a green emerald pendant.

"Coo. I'd rather like this for myself," she said to me, a funny glint in her eyes. "But it's marked seventy-five pounds. Do you reckon I could sneak it into my pocket before he comes back?"

I was so horrified I nearly screamed out loud.

"Put it down this minute, Angela Mitchell," I gasped, and luckily the man came squeaking back just then and she slid the necklace back into the cabinet. In the end we bought the painted wedding plate with Angela's fiver and my fifty pence, and the kind man wrapped the present in gift paper for us and tied it with ribbon.

"There," he said. "I hope the young couple will be very happy."

Off we went back to the bus stop, well pleased with our morning's work, although I had to wait a few minutes for Angela, who decided to stop just inside the shop doorway to tie her shoelace.

I chattered away cheerfully in the bus on the way home to Edgebourne, but Angela didn't say one single word. She sat as still as a stone, staring in front of her with the strangest expression, her face going paler and paler by the minute.

"Are you all right?" I said at last. "You look a bit sick."

"I feel a bit sick," she said faintly. "Oh, Charlie, I've done the most awful thing."

A police car overtook the bus just then, its siren blaring, and the bus had to pull over to let it past. To my complete astonishment, Angela dived onto the floor and tried to hide under the seat, only coming out when the police car was well past on its way to Edgebourne.

"Whatever's the matter with you?" I said, looking at her face, all red and flushed and scared-looking. "Anyone would think you were hiding from the police. You haven't robbed a bank or anything ... have ... you ...? Oh, blimey. Angela! How could you!"

The penny had suddenly dropped and I remembered the emerald pendant and the way she had hung back in the shop to bend down and tie her shoe.

"Don't tell anybody, Charlie," she whispered frantically. "I couldn't help it, honest. I don't know what came over me."

I grabbed her arm and stood up. "Come on, you!" I said. "We're getting off this bus right now and getting the next one straight back to Barlow. You can give the wretched thing back and just hope old hairy-nose won't call the police."

Angela cowered in her seat. "Please don't make me go back, Charlie," she begged. "I just couldn't. I'd die. I know I would. Anyway," she added, pulling me down into my seat again, "it's Wednesday, half-day closing, and by the time we wait for the next bus all the shops will be closed."

I plonked myself grimly back into my seat, and for the rest of the journey I thought about what she had done. I kept looking at her set face and her clenched hands and I began to wonder. I began to wonder if she was having me on, like the time she pretended to have kidnapped a baby from outside a supermarket, and it turned out it was her cousin Sarah Jane she was looking after for the afternoon. She's such a good actress that I can never tell whether she's telling the truth or a great big whopping fib. At last I thought of a way of catching her out.

"Let me see it, Angela," I demanded suddenly, and her eyes went huge and round.

"What, here?" she gulped, aghast. "You want me to show it to you on the bus, with everybody watching? You're even more stupid than I thought, Charlie Ellis. You haven't got the brain of a lettuce." And she slumped down into her coat collar and groaned quietly to herself until the bus arrived at the library corner where we get off.

"I'll just go and tell my mother that I'm back, and then I'll come round to your house," she said when she reached her gate. "You've got to help me decide what to do about this, Charlie. OK?"

"OK," I said wearily, and she gave me a

watery smile before disappearing down her drive and into the house.

When I got in Daniel was so ecstatic to see me that he almost licked my face off. My mum was in the kitchen making soup for lunch, and the smell was so wonderful I could almost forget Angela and her problems. But she turned up less than five minutes later and dragged me upstairs to my room.

The first thing I had to find out was whether the whole thing was just one of her stupid tricks, and she soon solved that by putting her hand in her pocket and flinging the gold and emerald necklace on my bed.

"There!" she said defiantly. "Now do you believe me?" And she fell down on the floor on my sheepskin rug and covered her face with her hands.

I stared at the necklace and swallowed hard. I had to believe her now, for there was the rotten thing to prove it. I tried to speak but nothing came out, except a sort of gargling noise.

Daniel bounced in, delighted to find Angela lying on the floor and convinced she was playing some sort of game.

"Gerroff, you stupid mutt!" she groaned, as he tugged at her hair with his teeth and tried to lick her face. "Gerrim off, for Pete's sake, Charlie! Look at the mess he's making of my hair."

I should have thought that was the least of her worries, but I bundled poor old Daniel out of the room and shut the door. Then I helped Angela to get up and sat her beside me on the bed.

We sat there gazing for ages into space and neither of us said a word. My brain just seemed to have seized up altogether and I hadn't a clue what to do. Once we heard a police car in the distance and we stared at each other and clutched each other's hand until it had gone past.

At last my mum called up the stairs that lunch was ready and did Angela want some too.

"Oh, no, thanks, Aunt Liz," Angela called back. "My mum's expecting me." And she shot out of my room and down the stairs, leaving the stolen necklace lying on my bed.

"OY! Just a minute!" I shouted. But it was too late. She had gone.

I gazed fearfully at the glittering emerald as

if it was burning a hole in the bedspread, then I quickly picked it up and hid it in one of my shoes in the wardrobe. Straight after lunch I'd take it back to her. She needn't think I was going to be a receiver of stolen goods.

My mum's home-made thick pea soup is delicious. It's got lovely chunks of pink ham in it, and we always have warm crusty bread to dunk in. But for once I couldn't eat a thing. All I could think of was that rotten necklace sitting in the bottom of my wardrobe like a skeleton in the cupboard and I knew I would have to get rid of it somehow. Maybe I could flush it down the loo, I thought, stirring my soup absently but not eating it.

"Not hungry, Charlie?" asked my mum in surprise. "I suppose you've been filling yourself up with rubbish in Barlow all morning."

I gave a sheepish grin and escaped upstairs as soon as I could. An idea was beginning to form in the back of my mind.

If I wrapped up the necklace and put it in an envelope, I could post it back to the shop. Then the man would have no idea who had stolen it, and he would probably be so pleased to get it back that he wouldn't bother mentioning it to the police at all. It was such a simple solution that I wondered why I hadn't thought of it before.

Feeling almost faint with relief, I wrote a little note on the small portable typewriter my Uncle Barrie had given me for Christmas in the hope that it would turn me into a famous writer one day.

So sorry, slipped this into my pocket by mistake while in your shop. Am returning it herewith, with apologies for any inconvenience.

I had to look up 'apologies' and 'inconvenience' in the posh new dictionary my Uncle Barrie had given me for Christmas (also in the hope that it would turn me into a famous writer one day).

I wrapped the necklace in a bit of tissue paper, folded the letter round it, and popped the whole lot into an envelope. Luckily I had noticed the name of the shop which was *Bygones*, so I addressed the envelope, 'The Proprietor, *Bygones*, Station Road, Barlow'. Then I stuffed it up my jumper and went downstairs to find my mum.

"Who're you writing to?" she asked curiously, when I begged for a first-class stamp.

"Anybody I know?" She laughed and rumpled my hair when I stammered and blushed, and told me not to worry, it was none of her business. I bet you anything she thought I was writing to that dishy David Watkins in my class at school who I've decided to marry when I grow up.

Anyway, she gave me the stamp and I grabbed my anorak and raced outside and down the street to the corner of the main road where the nearest pillar-box is. My fingers were shaking so much from cold and fright that I somehow got the stamp stuck on sideways. But at least it was on. And when I dropped the letter in the post-box I very nearly cried with relief. I couldn't wait to tell Angela what I'd done.

I raced back up the street, kicking up the snow and almost dancing for joy. I banged on Angela's door, shouting Angela's name and demanding to be let in at once.

Auntie Sally opened the door, and I could tell

she was still in the middle of lunch because she had her mouth so full she couldn't speak. She just waved me past her and pointed towards the kitchen.

But I stood for a moment rooted to the spot and totally unable to move, opening and shutting my mouth like a dying haddock, for hanging round Angela's mum's neck and sparkling prettily against her white fluffy sweater was an emerald pendant on a gold chain. Exactly like the one I'd just posted.

"What's the matter with you, Charlie?" she said impatiently, when she'd swallowed her mouthful of lunch. "Don't stand there like one o'clock half-struck. Come in, child."

I went into the kitchen and there was Angela shovelling sausages and chips and baked beans into her mouth as if she hadn't a care in the world.

"Sit down, Charlie," she said cheerfully. "We'll go for a walk when I've finished this."

Auntie Sally went back to the table and I watched them both eat for a moment. Then I cleared my throat.

"That's a very pretty necklace, Auntie

Sally," I said nervously. "Was it a Christmas present?"

Angela's mum gave one of her girlish giggles. "Good heavens, no!" she laughed. "It's not a real necklace at all. It came out of a Christmas cracker, one of those special ones from Harrods." She smiled across the table at Angela. "Angela's got one just like it, haven't you, darling?"

"I gave mine to Charlie," replied Angela with a grin, and when my slow brain had worked out just exactly what she meant I got up and walked behind her chair and before she could do anything to stop me I pushed her face straight down into her plate of sausages and beans and chips.

"Charlie!" she gasped, tomato sauce dripping off her chin, and Auntie Sally just sat there with her mouth hanging open, too astonished to say anything at all.

I took myself off home, put Daniel's lead on, and we went for a lovely long walk all by ourselves in the woods by the river. And every time I thought of Angela Mitchell sitting there at the table with tomato sauce dripping down her face I laughed so much I almost choked.

Chapter Three

THE sly cat, Angela, got her own back just two weeks later, at the wedding of Felicity Frensham-Pond, and I've never been so embarrassed in all my life. I've never seen my poor dad so embarrassed either, and that's what annoyed me more than anything. Angela plays her horrible stupid tricks on me so often that I've sort of got used to it, but when she starts doing it to my dad it's just not funny.

I had been quite looking forward to the

wedding, because my mum said I could put on my lovely new flame-coloured dress which I hadn't yet had a chance to wear. But of course the lousy January weather was so bad I had to have a coat over it to go to the church, but my best coat is short and a very bright shade of cherry red, and even I could see that the two colours clashed like cymbals in a brass band.

"Yuck," snorted Angela when she saw it. "Charlie Ellis, you've got about as much dress sense as a gooseberry flan."

She of course had yet another new outfit, a white wool dress with a gorgeous jewelled belt, and a matching white woollen cloak and hat. She had black shiny leather boots, a shiny leather handbag, and black gloves, and she looked like something off the front page of one of those fashion magazines they have in the waiting-room at the dentist. I kept my coat buttoned up tight and made up my mind to sit well away from her in church.

It was a very snowy morning and we had to go in two cars because there wasn't enough room for all of us in one. So Angela's dad took our two mums in his posh new Volvo so that their nice new clothes wouldn't get covered in dog hairs from the back seat of our car. My dad took me and Angela, and of course Angela wouldn't sit in the back either, so it was me that got covered in dog hairs.

But I suppose that was quite fair. As Angela pointed out, Daniel is my dog after all. And you should have seen his sad little face at the living-room window as we drove away, even though we had got Mrs Baines, his favourite doggy-sitter, in to look after him.

The church was packed when we got there. I looked around but we hardly knew anybody. Our family had only been invited because Felicity Frensham-Pond's mum had gone to school with my mum and I suppose she wanted everyone to see how she had gone up in the world. And you should have seen all the posh dresses and fur coats and the men in grey top hats and tail coats and the lot.

The bride came down the aisle on her father's arm and everybody went 'Ooh' and 'Aah' and 'Isn't she lovely!' although you couldn't see what she looked like at all because of the lace veil over her head. But at least nobody stood on her train and tripped her up which is what happened to my poor cousin Fiona at her wedding in Birmingham last year.

The ceremony wasn't quite as boring as usual, because the vicar started off by reading the burial service by mistake. Somebody had to tactfully point it out to him and after a lot of red-faced flapping through his book he found the right page and started all over again. That caused a bit of a giggle, although everybody tried to pretend they were only coughing in their hankies.

At last it was over and the organ music thundered out as we all piled outside for the photographs to be taken. But snow was coming down as if it was the North Pole and it was blowing such a blizzard that the photographer couldn't take any pictures at all.

"We'll just have to take them at the reception," he said, snowflakes sticking to his eyelashes and to his camera lens, and he hurried away to his car.

My mum and Auntie Sally scooted off with Uncle Jim in the Volvo, but before they left

Uncle Jim wound the window down to speak to my dad. "It's the Beaconsmead Hotel, Ted," he called out. "Make sure you ..." But the rest of what he said got blown away in the wind, and we scurried away to the car before we did, too.

It took us ages to get there. The snow was falling so thick and fast it clogged the windscreen wipers and my dad could hardly see where he was going.

"To think I'm missing the football match on the telly for this," he grumbled crossly. "Newcastle United are playing at Wembley."

Angela giggled. "You are silly, Uncle Ted," she told him. "If the snow's as bad as this there won't be any football on the telly. There'll be some soppy old film instead."

He couldn't think of an answer to that, and neither could I. She's always saying things that make you look stupid, and you feel like giving her a good kick on the shins because she always looks so smug and pleased with herself.

We arrived at the Beaconsmead Hotel at last and my dad drove into the car park.

"Now what?" he said. We all peered out and

saw a sign with two arrows on it. One arrow pointed left to the Windsor Suite, and the other pointed right to the Hampton Rooms.

"Left," said Angela quickly. "I'm sure my dad said it was the Windsor Suite." So we turned left and parked among the Rolls Royces and the Mercedes and the Jaguars and started to get the wedding presents out of the car.

I don't know why we had to carry them all, I'm sure, but for some reason they'd all been put into our car. There were two big parcels from Angela's mum and dad, one big parcel from mine, and the little parcel with the plate in it from me and Angela.

We dashed through the blizzard into the hotel with all these packages and a snooty young man at the reception desk helped us off with our snow-covered coats and frowned at the slushy mess we were making on his nice clean carpet.

"Windsor Suite?" asked my dad, picking up a couple of the parcels again, and the snooty receptionist jerked his thumb at the stairs.

"Up there," he said, so that's where we went.

A small orchestra was playing somewhere so

we followed the sound of the music until we found ourselves in a vast room like a cathedral, with gold cherubs all around the ceiling and beautiful paintings on the walls. Along one side of the room a buffet lunch was laid out, and my mouth watered when I saw all the yummy things there were to eat. A huge sideboard near the door had all the wedding presents arranged on it, and you should have seen the silver and the crystal and the embroidered linen and the piles of parcels wrapped in pretty wedding paper and ribbon still waiting to be opened.

We dumped our presents on the end of the sideboard. Then my dad grabbed a glass of champagne from a tray and we went to look for our mums and Angela's dad.

We could see a queue of people forming, waiting to kiss and congratulate the bride and groom, so we joined on the end of that, but there was no sign of our mums anywhere. In fact we didn't recognise one single person in that room, and nobody seemed to be taking the slightest notice of us.

At last we reached the bride. My dad stepped forward, handing me his glass of champagne to hold, which gave Angela and me a chance to have a quick swig when he wasn't looking.

"Congratulations, my dear," my dad mumbled at the bride, taking her hand. "I hope you'll both be very happy." He kissed the plump and pretty dark-haired girl on the cheek, shook hands with the young groom and then we moved away, with Angela and me bobbing a sort of quick curtsey.

I saw that Angela was gazing at the bride with a horrified look on her face. She tugged frantically at my dad's arm and dragged us both into a corner beside a pink velvet curtain.

"That's not Felicity Frensham-Pond," she hissed urgently. "I'm sure it isn't. I haven't seen her since I was little, but her mother keeps sending us photos of her." She stared hard at the bride and groom, who were whispering together and looking at us curiously. "Felicity Frensham-Pond is blonde, for a start," declared Angela. "She's also six feet tall. And she's as skinny as a hockey stick turned sideways."

My dad groaned and clutched at his tie, which seemed to be strangling him. "Maybe there are two weddings," he said. "We must have come to the wrong reception. Maybe we should have gone to that other place, what was it called?"

"The Hampton Rooms," said Angela, and I saw that her eyes had gone that funny green colour they go when she's up to mischief. "That's probably what my dad was trying to tell us when we left the church," she said. "He was shouting something out of the car window."

My dad sighed. "Never mind," he said. "There's no harm done, I suppose. We'll just sneak out and go to the other one. Nobody seems to have noticed us here."

I wasn't so sure. I had just seen the bridegroom beckoning to two great hefty blokes in brown suits who looked like gorillas, with great long arms that almost touched the ground. They both looked as if they could tie their shoelaces without bending down.

The bridegroom spoke to them quietly and they looked in our direction, then they started crossing the room towards us just as my dad decided to sneak off towards the door.

"Come on, girls," he said over his shoulder. "The sooner we get out of here the better."

We hurried after him and had almost escaped when my dad clapped his hand to his brow.

"The wedding presents!" he groaned. "Oh, lord. We can't go without the wedding presents. Your mother would kill me."

We rushed over to the sideboard, but other people had arrived after us and it was so piled up with parcels that we couldn't see which were ours. We had to rummage about until we spotted the right labels, and by then the two men in brown were almost on top of us.

We each grabbed a parcel or two and ran once again for the door, and all of a sudden it was like a scene from one of those crime films on the telly. A fat lady in a flowered costume that made her look like an overstuffed sofa cried out, "Stop them! They're pinching the wedding presents!" And that's when everybody started yelling and screaming, and a boy with red curly hair and freckles and strawberry mousse all round his mouth stuck out his foot and tripped me up and sent me flying across the floor, and somebody else grabbed Angela who screamed louder than anybody, and the two burly blokes in brown each grabbed one of my dad's arms and slammed him up against the wall so hard you could hear the breath being knocked out of his body.

"Nah, then?" they demanded, poking my dad in the ribs. "What do you think you're up to, then? Helping yourself to the silver, eh?" And my poor dad just went scarlet in the face and gaped in astonishment and couldn't say a single word.

Angela and I were brought forward and pushed against the wall as well, and I was so scared my teeth wobbled.

"Here's his accomplices," said the red-haired boy who'd tripped me up. "I saw them both taking things." He was holding my wrist so tight that he was hurting me, so I kicked him hard on the ankle to make him let go.

"Here!" he said. "Did you see that, everybody? Assault as well as burglary!"

My dad gave me a warning look so I calmed down a bit and contented myself with sticking my tongue out at the boy as far as it would go.

Somebody went off to phone the police and it was then that Angela started having hysterics. "I'm innocent!" she cried out piteously, like Oliver Twist which we'd seen on the telly the week before. "They made me do it, honest!" And of course that didn't help at all.

The two blokes in brown, who turned out to be hotel security guards, wanted us all locked up in the manager's office until the police arrived. My dad began shouting above the noise, trying to explain that we'd made a terrible mistake, but nobody took the slightest notice of him in the least. It was all like some horrible nightmare, but no matter how hard I pinched myself I still didn't wake up, so I knew that it was real all right.

Suddenly there was a commotion near the door and a loud commanding voice was heard bellowing above the din.

"What on earth is going on here, may I ask?" Everybody fell back to let through this enormous tall woman in a purple velvet dress and a huge picture hat who acted like she owned the place. I almost cried with relief when I realised who she was because there behind her was my mum and Angela's mum and Angela's dad. They'd guessed that we'd gone to the wrong reception and they'd all come to look for us. They looked perfectly astounded to see what was going on and the purple lady, who turned out to be Mrs Frensham-Pond herself, demanded our release immediately.

Angela flung herself at her mother and boo-hooed like a five-year-old into her mum's new pink satin suit, and Angela's mum stroked Angela's blond hair and said, "There, there, darling. Everything's all right now. Mummy's here." And Angela turned her head slightly and gave me such an enormous wink that I began to wonder whether she'd planned the whole thing all along.

Well, after a lot of argument the purple lady finally convinced them that it had been a genuine mistake and they let us go. Mrs Frensham-Pond swept majestically out and we trooped sheepishly along behind her, after picking up the wretched wedding presents which I never wanted to see again as long as I lived.

Of course we had just reached the corridor when two uniformed policemen arrived, and the whole thing had to be explained all over again. They stared at us very hard and looked dead disappointed that they weren't going to arrest anybody after all, but somebody gave them a glass of champagne which cheered them up even though everybody knows they're not supposed to drink on duty.

We got to the right reception at long last, but by then my dad and I were feeling so shaken and upset we hadn't a hope of enjoying ourselves. In any case all the best food had gone by then and there were only a few cheese sandwiches with their corners curling up and some cold sausage rolls with that thick soggy pastry that sticks to the roof of your mouth so that you can't speak for five whole minutes.

Angela wasn't upset at all, of course. She danced about, showing off as usual, telling everybody about how we had nearly got arrested and making everybody laugh with her description of my poor dad being slammed against the wall. Uncle Jim thought the whole thing was hilarious.

"I still don't know how you went to the wrong rooms," he said, waving a glass of champagne around and grinning all over his face. "Even if you didn't hear me shouting from the car, I'm sure Angela knew it was the Hampton Rooms you wanted." He turned to Angela, who was flirting with a handsome boy with a carnation in his button-hole. "I told you, darling, didn't I?" he said. "Before we left?"

Everybody looked at Angela and I thought my dad was going to burst, but he only swallowed a large mouthful of champagne and banged the glass down so hard that everything on the table rattled.

Angela looked at her dad and gave him one of her dazzling smiles that would melt the heart of a snowman.

"Did you, Dad?" she said sweetly. "Oh dear. I'm sorry. I don't think I heard you." And off she floated, to go and dance with her new boyfriend.

I didn't dance once at that wedding, even though lots of dishy boys came and asked me and I knew I looked great in my flame-coloured dress. All I did was sit in the corner and scowl, and rack my brains for revenge.

Chapter Four

ALTHOUGH my dad calls her a fiend, Angela isn't horrible all the time. Sometimes she has some really great ideas. And she can be quite unselfish when she wants to be. Like the time she planned that jumble sale to help the poor children in Africa. It wasn't her fault about the committee room carpet. Well, I don't think it was, anyway.

It was a bright spring Saturday morning and I was sitting in the garden trying to teach Daniel to sit up and beg for a biscuit. I was getting all hot and bothered because I wasn't having any success at all. Daniel only has to see a biscuit and he starts bouncing up and down like a yo-yo. Angela says we should feed him properly and then he wouldn't have to eat like a starving Hoover, but my dad says if we fed him any more he'd burst.

Daniel didn't seem to be getting the idea about begging, so I thought it would help if I showed him exactly what I meant. I balanced a biscuit on my nose and sat and begged like the poodle I'd seen on 'That's My Dog' on the telly.

Daniel stared at me for a moment with his head on one side. Then he launched himself straight at my face like a missile, knocking me flat on my back and racing off round the lawn with the biscuit in his teeth.

Of course Angela came round the corner of the house just at that very moment and saw the whole thing, and it took her almost five minutes to stop laughing and tell me what she'd come round for.

I went indoors and got two glasses of lemonade while she recovered, and when I came back she was sitting on the rug trying to balance a biscuit on Daniel's nose.

"He's the thickest dog I've ever met," she said in disgust. "Do you know what? If they had a competition for the most stupid dog in the whole world he'd be sure to win first prize." Daniel licked her face and wagged his tail in delight at the compliment.

As we drank our lemonade in the sunshine she started telling me about this wonderful idea she'd had in the middle of the night and how she'd been so thrilled about it she hadn't had a wink of sleep.

"You know that appeal there was on the telly last night?" she said, picking daisies off the lawn and starting to make a chain of them. "Asking school kids to raise money from fairs and sponsored swims and stuff, and sending it all to the famine countries?"

"Yes, I saw it," I said, starting a daisy-chain of my own. "What about it?"

Angela looked me straight in the eyes, the way she does when she wants to convince me about something. "Well, we could do it!" she said.

I blinked a bit and stared at her.

"Who?" I said. "Us? Why us? The whole school is already having a big appeal and a fair and everything. What can you and I do?"

"We could do something on our own," she said, her blue eyes sparkling excitedly. "Just the two of us. We could organise it ourselves and do everything ourselves and it would be all our own work."

Then her voice went all noble and full of self-sacrifice, as if she was giving her last scrap of bread to a hungry beggar. "It would prove that ordinary kids like you and me really care about our starving brothers and sisters," she said solemnly. I found it very hard not to laugh, but she looked so serious I didn't dare.

Her face was getting pinker and pinker the more excited she got. "We'd raise pots of money, Charlie, honest," she said. "And we might get our photos in the local papers."

Her eyes suddenly went round as saucers. "We might even get on the telly, like that Bob What'sisname!"

"He happened to raise several million

pounds," I said sarcastically. "How do you expect to match that?"

Angela finished making her daisy necklace and hung it round Daniel's neck. He gave one of his dopey grins and went galloping round and round the lawn like a circus pony. Then he lay down and started shredding the daisy-chain into tiny bits with his teeth.

"That's gratitude for you," grumbled Angela, watching him. "Anyway, Charlie, we don't have to raise millions. It's not the amount that counts. It's just to show that we care enough to do it. Don't you see?"

And in the end she got her own way as usual. I agreed to help, not just to please her but because I thought it was a great idea anyway and I was astonished that she'd thought of it.

So for the rest of the morning we sat there with a notebook and pencil and made some plans. We decided a jumble sale was the answer, because people would always rather give rubbish away than money, and sponsored walks and swims and things are getting a bit overdone in our area.

Once we'd decided that, the rest of it was

easy. All we needed were some slips of paper, asking for jumble and telling people about the appeal.

"We can keep all the stuff in our two garages until the day," said Angela. "And we'll have to get our dads to help. If there's a lot of big stuff we may even have to hire a van to take it to the hall." She really was getting carried away by the whole thing.

"Hall?" I said. "What hall? Where are we going to have this jumble sale, Angela Mitchell? The Community Centre's far too big, and anyway it costs a fortune to hire."

"Oh, crumbs!" she said. "I never thought of that." And she lay down on the grass and stared at the sky for such a long time I thought she'd fallen asleep.

"I've got it!" she said at last, sitting bolt upright and giving me a grin. "What about the committee room at the Community Centre? There's a huge table in there to put the stuff on, and there's that little kitchen place where we can sell cups of tea and buns and things. It's perfect, Charlie. Just the right size and every-thing."

"And who's going to let us use the committee room?" I asked gloomily, my heart suddenly sinking like my Granny Ellis's fruitcake because I knew what was coming next. "It's only meant to be used for local council meetings and things like that."

Angela jumped up and dragged me to my feet. "Exactly!" she crowed. "And who do we know on the local council? Your dad's brother, your Uncle David, who's so soppy about you he could never refuse you a thing!"

It was no use arguing with her. Off she danced to go and get the leaflets printed on her dad's word-processor, leaving me sunk in gloom.

"We'll have another meeting tomorrow, Charlie," she said importantly as she left. "We can report to each other on our progress."

My dad came home from his tennis match with Uncle Jim, and he'd brought fish and chips back like he usually does on a Saturday lunch-time to give my mum a break from cooking.

"What's the matter, bonny lass?" he asked me, as I picked slowly at my slice of cod. "Is this the face that launched a thousand chips?"

"Angela's been here all morning," said my

mum, buttering a slice of bread. "She hasn't been upsetting you, has she, Charlie?"

So in the end I told them both the whole story, and they listened without saying a word until I'd finished.

"Blimey!" said my dad at last. "Angela thought of that all by herself? That kid's certainly full of surprises."

He got up from the table and went to the phone, and after a minute or two I could hear him arguing.

"What harm would it do, David?" he was saying. "I think it's a most commendable idea myself. Especially when you think what sort of a kid this Angela is. And I know Charlie would be really grateful." He turned and winked at me and suddenly gave a thumbs-up signal. "Carpet?" he said into the phone. "What carpet? Oh, that carpet. Yes, of course. OK. I'll tell her. Right. Many thanks, David. 'Bye."

He put the phone down and came back to the table all smiles. And I suddenly got back my appetite and started tucking in to my fish and chips, all smothered in yummy tomato ketchup.

"No problem, Charlie," grinned my dad. "Uncle David wants to know the date of the sale as soon as possible, of course, so he can keep the room free. And he wants you to roll up the new carpet and stick it away somewhere. It's ten metres by five and cost almost three hundred pounds, and he doesn't want dirty feet tramping in and out on it all day. All right?"

"All right, Dad," I mumbled gratefully, my mouth full of chips. "I'll make sure the carpet gets put somewhere safe."

"You'd better, kid," said my dad. "He's holding me responsible for it, so I don't want anything happening to the blooming thing."

Angela was delighted with the news when she came round the next morning. "I knew you'd persuade him, Charlie," she said, and she was so pleased with me she took both my hands and danced me all round the apple tree, which made Daniel bark his head off in astonishment.

I somehow didn't have the heart to tell her it was my dad who had done it all. I just explained about the new committee room carpet, and then we set off to deliver the leaflets.

"What are we going all this way for?" I complained, as she led me down to the riverside and into the posh Abbotsmead estate. "Why can't we just put the leaflets in the houses round our way?"

Angela gave me a disgusted look. "People round our way will only give us cheap rubbish," she said. "The people who live round here are well-off, and all their rubbish will be posh rubbish. Just you wait and see."

And as usual, she was quite right. The stuff started arriving the very next day. And my eyes almost popped out of my head when I saw the fur coats and silk dresses and nice soft jumpers and evening wear and frilly shirts and men's suits and china ornaments and silver cutlery and pots and pans and pictures and paintings and books and records and binoculars and more books and more records and hats with feathers on and hundreds of pairs of shoes and more records and even a record-player and a million more books. Most of the clothes were better than the ones in my wardrobe, but that rotten Angela wouldn't let me keep one single thing.

Anyway, after about ten days both our garages were so full we couldn't get the cars in, so we thought it was about time we decided on the big day.

We chose a Saturday afternoon. A lot of people go shopping on Saturdays and would be tempted to call in at our sale. We painted some colourful posters and stuck them all over the town, and we printed more leaflets and put them through people's doors.

My dad fixed the date with Uncle David, and was snorting with laughter when he came back from the phone.

"Your Uncle David says he's solved that terrible dandruff problem he had," he said. "The poor guy's lost all his hair!"

"I hope he's not worrying about the committee room carpet," I said. "I've promised to look after it, and so has Angela."

"Don't worry, pet," laughed my dad. "David's only kidding. I'm sure nothing will go wrong."

The great day arrived at last. The sale was due to start at two o'clock, so my dad and Uncle Jim worked all morning moving the stuff to the Community Centre, using a small van hired from a local firm.

My mum and I baked cakes and scones all morning, and by the time we arrived at the Community Centre the sale was just about to start. Angela's mum was making tea in the little side-kitchen, and people were already crowding into the committee room, rummaging about and squabbling over bargains.

We had all agreed that only Angela and I would do the actual selling, so that we could say it was all our own work, and when I went into the committee room there was Angela, her face all flushed and excited, stuffing money into a sort of leather pouch she had tied round her waist.

"Thank goodness you're here, Charlie," she said when she saw me. "I can't cope with this lot on my own." She opened the pouch to show me the money. "It's going great. Look how much we've got already. I got five pounds for that old green carpet."

At first I just opened my mouth and stared at her as if I couldn't believe my ears. I felt as if somebody was sliding frozen fish fingers down the back of my neck.

"W ... what carpet?" I said at last, my voice

coming out like a cat's when you tread on its tail. Angela grinned happily.

"Oh, just some old carpet that was rolled up in the corner. Jenny Baker and her husband bought it for their new flat. They weren't half pleased with it, I can tell you!"

She turned to serve an irate lady who was banging on the table for attention, and I charged like a mad bull through the crowd towards the door. I felt like murdering Angela, but that would have to wait. What mattered was getting that carpet back before anybody realised it was missing.

Luckily I knew the librarian Jenny Baker well, and she had already told me about her new flat in Fowler Gardens. She was such a nice person I was sure she would understand about the carpet being sold by mistake, so I raced down the street and round the corner to Number 5 and started banging frantically on the front door. After a minute or two a ginger-bearded young man with a Stanley knife in his hand came to the door and I guessed it must be Jenny's husband, although I'd never seen him before. Anyway, before he even said one word I almost screamed with horror because behind him on the hall floor I could see a roll of dark green carpet that he had been *cutting into pieces*.

"Er ... is that the carpet you've just bought at the jumble sale, Mr Baker?" I managed to stammer, and he grinned with pleasure.

"Yes, we got a real bargain. It'll fit the stairs a treat once I finish cutting it into strips."

He stared at me. "Hey, are you all right, kid?" he said anxiously. "Your face is the colour of scrambled eggs. Do you want to come in and sit down for a minute?"

"I'll be all right," I said, hurriedly backing away from the door. I wanted to get as far away from that carpet as possible, and never see it again.

He shrugged and shut the door. I stood in the street, wondering what to do next. What I really wanted to do was run home and hide in the garden shed and not come out until bed-time, but that wouldn't solve anything. After dithering about for a few minutes I decided the only thing to do was to try to find my dad. He was the only person in the world I dared confess this mess to.

Well, it didn't take long to find him, for suddenly there he was walking round the corner after taking the van back to the hire firm, and the first thing he did when he saw my face was make me sit down on a bench in the street and tell him all about it.

When I'd finished telling him about the Baker's lovely new stair carpet, I realised just what Mr Baker meant by scrambled eggs because my dad's face had gone that exact same shade of pale lumpy yellow.

He stared at his shoes for a minute. Then he cleaned his glasses on a very dirty hanky which probably smeared them worse than before. Then he got up and pulled me to my feet.

"Come on, Charlie," he said. "There's only one thing to do. We'll have to buy a new one. We can't let Uncle David down, can we?"

I very nearly cried with relief as my dad hurried me back to the car park and bundled me into the car and we drove like demons along the road to Barlow, where they've got the biggest carpet shop in the whole world. They've got every size and colour you can think of, and I knew we would get what we wanted there.

"This is going to make a great big hole in our holiday savings," sighed my dad as we went into the shop, and I very nearly cried all over again because he's the best dad anybody ever had and he hadn't once told me off about what had happened, even though he must have been hopping mad.

I forgot about crying as soon as I looked at the first row of carpets hanging up. There was the exact shade of dark green I'd seen Mr Baker cutting up with his Stanley knife.

"That's it, Dad," I said excitedly, pointing to the green carpet. "I'm sure that's the right colour."

I looked at my dad because he wasn't saying anything at all. He was staring at me with a most peculiar expression on his face.

"Wh . . . what's the matter, Dad?" I faltered. "Are you all right?"

"Charlie, my bonny lass," he said, slowly and carefully as if he was talking to a half-wit. "Let me get this straight. The carpet Angela sold to the Baker couple was green, right?"

"Yes, Dad," I said. "I'm positive it was. I saw Mr Baker cutting it up."

My dad tugged at his hair until it was all standing on end, which was a mistake because he hasn't got much left anyway. Then he jammed his cheque book back into his pocket as if it was trying to jump out again, grabbed my arm and dragged me out of the shop.

"The committee room carpet isn't green, Charlie," he growled into my ear. "It's red! At least it was when I rolled it up this morning! Somebody's playing silly beggars, and I've a jolly good idea who it is!"

He drove back to the Community Centre in Edgebourne so fast it was like flying, and we burst into the committee room together.

By now the sale was almost over. A couple of disappointed old ladies were half-heartedly turning over a few pairs of woolly knickers, but all the best bargains had obviously gone. Through the serving hatch I could see my mum and Auntie Sally washing up mountains of cups and saucers, and giggling like schoolgirls together over the pile of money they had made.

Angela, flushed and triumphant and almost staggering under the weight of her money-bag, was having her photo taken by a photographer from the local paper, while a short tubby reporter who looked like Winnie-the-Pooh made notes in a notebook.

"All by yourself?" he was saying incredulously. "You organised all this by yourself? You must be some kid!"

"Well, I did have some help from my parents, of course," Angela said modestly. "And I had a friend who was supposed to be helping me. But she disappeared somewhere just after it started."

My dad folded his arms and glared at her grimly.

"All right, Angela," he said, scowling like our teacher does when you haven't done your homework. "Where is it?"

Angela turned to him in surprise. "Where's what, Uncle Ted?" she said, all innocent. "What are you looking so upset about?"

"THE COMMITTEE ROOM CARPET!" shouted my dad. "Where is it, girl? Charlie thought you had sold it!"

Angela gave a giggle just like one of her mother's and tossed her head. Then she walked over to a cupboard in the corner and flung it open. And there in the cupboard, rolled up like a big red sausage, was the committee room carpet, safe and sound.

"Silly Charlie," grinned Angela. "You didn't really think I'd sold it, did you? It's been in there all the time."

I didn't half feel stupid, I can tell you. But there wasn't a thing I could do. And I still don't know to this day whether she let me make that mistake on purpose.

One thing I do know, though. She got every scrap of credit for the sale. It was splashed all over the front page of the local paper a few days later, with a great big photo of Angela, smiling all over her face.

"Village girl raises five hundred pounds for charity single-handed!" it said, in letters two inches tall. My mum and dad and I all sat and read it together at the kitchen table, and for the first time in her life my mum said a very rude word.

Chapter Five

ANGELA and I had just set off for school one morning when we saw a farm lorry coming slowly along the street with a large and very smelly load of horse-manure on the back.

"Pooh!" said Angela, putting her hanky over her nose. "What a stink! Mr Willick must have ordered it for his potato patch. So now we'll have to keep all our windows shut for weeks."

Mr Willick lives next door to Angela on the other side from us, and he's a very keen gardener. He wins prizes in all the shows for his onions and his leeks and his strawberries and things, but somehow you don't feel like eating them when you see the sort of stuff he feeds them on.

Anyway, it looked as if the driver of this lorry hadn't delivered to Mr Willick before, because he was leaning out of his cab, trying to find the right house. Then he spotted me and Angela with our school uniforms and satchels and gave us a wave.

"Hey!" he called. "Do you kids know which is Mr Willick's house? They forgot to tell me the number back at the farm."

I opened my mouth to speak, but Angela pinched my arm so hard I almost squealed.

"You're at the wrong end of the street," she told the man, grinning one of her cheeky grins that make all her dimples show. "Mr Willick lives down there at Number 17. The house with the shiny red gates."

"Thanks a lot," smiled the driver. He pulled away from the kerb and drove down the street towards Number 17.

I stared at Angela stupidly for a moment.

How could she make such a mistake? Miss Menzies lives at Number 17, and she certainly wouldn't want a load of dirty stuff like horse-manure. She's the cleanest lady I've ever seen, as well as being the fattest, and she spends all her time when she's not eating, cleaning her windows, polishing her garden gnomes and sweeping every speck of dust from her drive. She's got the neatest and tidiest front garden in the street, and the most boring.

It was only when I saw Angela's gleeful face as the lorry backed through the red gates and tipped all that slimy stuff into Miss Menzies' drive, that I realised that she hadn't made a mistake at all.

We hurried past, keeping our heads well down, just as Miss Menzies appeared at the door in her dressing-gown and curlers, her fat face red and astonished, and all her twelve chins wobbling in fury.

"Angela!" I scolded, as we turned the corner safely out of sight. "That was a rotten thing to do. Especially to somebody like Miss Menzies, who likes everything so clean and nice."

Angela, totally unrepentant, did a crazy sort of dance along the street.

"It serves her right," she said. "The woman's potty. She told me off the other day for putting my sticky fingers on her stupid shiny gates." She grinned at my disapproving face. "Miss Menzies really does go too far, Charlie," she said. "I bet she even wears her apron in bed in case she gets her nightie dirty."

Snorting with laughter at this ludicrous picture, Angela ran off towards the school, with me following along behind, trying not to giggle.

Angela always likes to get her own back on anybody who upsets her, even if it's only for the slightest reason. She once tied her dad's shoelaces together while he was snoozing in a deckchair in the garden, just because he wouldn't buy her an ice-cream. Then she shouted in his ear that his boss wanted him on the telephone and poor Uncle Jim leaped up and fell flat on his face into the fishpond. She didn't get into trouble, though. Uncle Jim laughed about it for days afterwards, telling all his friends and shaking his head and saying things like, "What a kid" and "What a little rascal!", as if she was only five years old.

So that's why I wasn't a bit surprised at school that day when Angela took me to one side at break-time and told me her plan to mess up Miss Sopwith's dancing display. I knew Miss Sopwith had annoyed her, and I knew that Angela wouldn't rest until she got her own back.

It was during the morning Nature lesson that it had happened. Old Soppy thought it would be a good idea if we each stood up one at a time and told the rest of the class about something we had noticed at the weekend. Something that showed us spring was here, she said. It was just the sort of soppy idea old Soppy is always coming up with, and after all the usual moans and groans had quietened down she started with me.

I was lucky because we've got a pond in our garden that gets full of frogs at this time of year, so I told the class about the frogspawn, and about how it was just beginning to hatch into tadpoles, and they all yawned and groaned some more because they'd all heard about it a hundred times already.

"Thank you, Charlotte," said Miss Sopwith when I sat down. "That was most interesting. Now, what about you, Angela? What signs of spring did you see this weekend?"

Angela is about as interested in Nature as fish are interested in motorbikes, so she immediately went red and ummed and erred like an actor who's forgotten his lines. She looked desperately at me for help, and I suddenly remembered our walk along the riverbank on Sunday afternoon. I quickly mouthed the words 'swan's nest' and 'cygnets' at her behind my hand.

Angela beamed as she got the message. She cleared her throat importantly and looked around at the expectant faces of the class.

"On Sunday," she said loudly, "Charlie and I went for a walk along the Thames. We saw a swan's nest. And it had four baby signals in it."

She sat down abruptly as Laurence Parker started to hoot and jeer, and pretty soon the whole class was giggling like mad, especially that silly idiot Jenny Blake.

Angela sat stony-faced while even Miss Sopwith joined in the laughter.

"Were they railway signals, Angela?" she

chuckled, and I thought, 'Uh-oh! I wouldn't like to be you, Miss Sopwith', because I knew by Angela's expression that she was already planning her revenge.

It was during break that Angela told me what she was plotting to do. Old Soppy is very keen on country dancing, and several weeks earlier she had chosen a team of eight of us to demonstrate what we had learnt to the rest of the school. Angela and I were both in the team, and the dance we had to demonstrate was a complicated thing called the Cumberland Square Eight which can end up in a terrible mess if everybody doesn't keep their wits about them. We had been rehearsing the wretched thing for weeks until we were sick to death of it, but now we could all do it perfectly, and the demonstration was planned for Friday afternoon in the school hall.

Angela could hardly tell me for laughing, but when I finally understood what she wanted us to do I was horrified.

"No," I said firmly. "Not blooming likely. We'll all get into trouble and be the laughing stock of the whole school. You can mess the thing up yourself if you want to, but leave me out of it if you don't mind." I tried to walk away from her but she caught hold of my arm.

"Don't spoil everything, Charlie," she said. "I'm going to ask all the others in the team as well. Then we'll all be in it together and nobody will get the blame." She put on her pleading look like Daniel does when you're stuffing your very last bit of sausage in your mouth.

"Oh, come on, Charlie," she coaxed. "Be a sport. We'll do it when we get to that eightsome reel bit. Everybody will set off in the wrong direction and it'll be an absolute shambles in no time. Just think of old Soppy's face!"

I still didn't like it much, but if all eight of us were going to be involved it wouldn't be so bad, I supposed. One person couldn't get the blame if the whole dance went wrong. So I reluctantly agreed, offering to go with her to tell all the other members of the team about it.

"You're great, Charlie!" she said, her eyes sparkling in delight. "I was sure you'd be an old fuddley-duddley and say no. You can be a real sport sometimes, you know." And I couldn't help grinning at her and feeling dead pleased at her praise, even though she wouldn't let me go with her to tell the others.

"It would look too suspicious," she explained. "Old Soppy is on playground duty and might notice something. No, Charlie. I'll just slip round on my own and let everybody know."

She gave my hand a quick squeeze and ran off. I sat on the wall in the sun and watched her as she went round all the members of the team one at a time and whispered in their ears. I saw them all giggle and nod excitedly, and each one of them looked over at me where I was sitting on the wall. I winked and grinned and waved, to show I was in on it too, which seemed to make them giggle all the harder, for some reason that I couldn't fathom.

The last person Angela spoke to was Jenny Blake, and I thought that was a bit strange because Jenny wasn't even on the demonstration team. But she and Angela had sort of ganged up together since we moved up to Miss Sopwith's class, and I supposed Angela just wanted to tell her what was going on.

Anyway, Angela came back after a while and

said everybody had agreed, and they were all coming round to her house after school for a rehearsal.

So at four o'clock we all set off for Angela's, and took our positions for the Cumberland Square Eight on Angela's back lawn. And even I had to laugh when we all deliberately got tangled up in the middle of the eightsome reel. Some went off in one direction, some went off in another. David Watkins just hopped up and down on the spot in the middle, and Angela and I got so wound around each other that we actually fell over in a heap on the lawn. In the end we were all shrieking and shouting and giggling so much that Auntie Sally came out to see what was going on.

"We're rehearsing our dance, Mum," spluttered Angela, struggling to her feet and falling over again. "We're giving a demonstration to the rest of the school on Friday."

Auntie Sally gave a snort of disgust. "I'm sure they'll be most impressed," she said, and she went back into the kitchen.

Well, of course that made us laugh even more, and I was still laughing about it when I went home. All the time I was eating my lamb chop and mashed potatoes and peas I kept exploding into little giggles, and I could see my mum and dad raising their eyebrows at one another and shaking their heads.

"Are you all right, Charlie?" my dad said at last. "I didn't know lamb chops were as funny as all that."

"It's OK, Dad," I said. "It's just a little joke we're planning for Friday afternoon." My giggles turned to hiccups and I had to go and get a drink of water to settle them down. When I got back to the table my mum and dad were looking rather serious, like they do when they're discussing my school report or the telephone bill.

"This joke you're planning, Charlie," said my dad. "It's not one of Angela's barmy ideas, is it?" And when I said it was he looked even more serious.

"I wouldn't get involved, if I were you," he warned. "You know how she has a habit of somehow putting all the blame on you."

"Not this time, Dad," I smiled confidently. "There's a lot of us in it together." And I scooted off upstairs to do my homework before they could ask me any more questions.

Friday came at last, and Miss Sopwith asked the dancing team to meet her in the assembly hall after lunch for a final rehearsal. We got into our positions on the stage while old Soppy started the cassette player and we performed the dance absolutely perfectly. Not one of us made a mistake and the eightsome reel went like a dream. A loud chord of music ended the dance, we all bowed to our partners and Miss Sopwith clapped her hands until they must have been sore.

"That was beautiful, boys and girls," she beamed, and I could have sworn she even had tears in her eyes. "I'm very pleased with you indeed. If you dance like that this afternoon, Miss Collingwood will be delighted."

My heart turned cold and sank like an ice cube in a glass of lemonade. Miss Collingwood is the headmistress, and while being kind and extremely fair, she hates to see anyone fooling about. "Be dignified, and be a credit to your school," she's always telling us in assembly. I knew she wouldn't appreciate Angela's version of the Cumberland Square Eight at all.

But there was no time to tell Angela my fears, for just then the bell rang for afternoon school to begin and all the classes started filing in one at a time and sitting in rows on the floor. Finally the whole school had assembled and were all sitting there staring up at us on the stage and whispering and sniggering as if we were waxworks at Madame Tussaud's and I felt dead nervous, I can tell you.

I felt even more nervous when all the teachers walked in and sat down on a line of chairs in the middle of the front row. They left the centre one empty, and all at once the whispering and sniggering stopped like magic and Miss Collingwood swept majestically into the hall and took her place.

She smiled round at everybody, then nodded to Miss Sopwith, who was standing on the corner of the stage. Miss Sopwith cleared her throat and stepped forward.

"Good afternoon, everybody," she said.

"The demonstration dance team will now perform for you the Cumberland Square Eight."

We quickly took our positions and Angela gave my arm a squeeze as we passed. "I'm counting on you, Charlie," she whispered, and I heaved a great sigh. There was no getting out of it now.

Miss Sopwith switched on the tape and we all bowed to our partners as a loud chord of music filled the hall. Then the dance began and for the first few minutes we danced as we had never danced before. I could see old Soppy smiling proudly, and Miss Collingwood in the front row tapping the floor with her foot in time to the beat.

Then it happened. "Now!" hissed Angela into my ear as the music changed and we went into the complicated steps of the eightsome reel. So instead of turning left to swing round my partner, I turned right and bumped into the person behind me. Then I turned left again and bumped into somebody else. I went on like this, bumping into everybody I could see, finally jigging round and round in the middle of the dance as if I'd been at my Grandad's home-made elderberry wine.

I grinned at Angela as she danced past, expecting her to grin back, but to my astonishment her face was dead serious and she wouldn't even look at me. I looked at all the others' faces and I felt as cold as the North Pole when I saw what was happening. They were all doing their best to keep the eightsome reel going in spite of my messing around, and *not one of them was putting a foot wrong, not even Angela!*

By now the sniggering had started somewhere in the middle of the hall, and it wasn't long before it spread round the whole school. My face went all red and horrified, the sniggering grew louder until it turned into great hoots and bellows of laughter, and nobody could hear the music anymore.

Miss Sopwith, her face as red as mine, quickly switched off the music. Then she marched up on the stage and yanked me out of the middle of the team of dancers. She turned to face the school, holding my arm as if I was a criminal trying to escape.

"I'm sorry, Miss Collingwood," she blurted out. "Charlie doesn't seem to have had enough practice. We'll start the dance again, if you don't mind. Jenny Blake, will you please come and take Charlie's place?"

I had to go and sit on the floor and watch while that stupid kid danced in my place. And you can guess how furious I was when I found she could do it beautifully. Angela must have been secretly coaching her for weeks.

So that's how I lost my place on the dancing team, all because of Angela and her rotten scheme. She swore afterwards that everybody had changed their minds at the last minute and there hadn't been time to tell me. She crossed her heart and hoped to die that it hadn't been a deliberate plot to get her new friend on the team instead of me. But I know better. And one of these days I'm really going to get my own back.

Chapter Six

ANGELA thought it was the funniest thing that ever happened when somebody stole my dad's car.

"I don't believe it!" she giggled. "Why on earth would anybody want to pinch a tatty old thing like that? It was only fit for the scrap-heap, anyway."

My dad and I didn't think it was funny at all. We've had our old Morris for so long that it seems like one of the family, and to think that some yobs might be driving it around and maybe even smashing it up almost brought tears to our eyes.

It was while we were having lunch at a seaside café that it happened. The weather was so nice one day in the half-term holidays that my dad offered to take Angela and me and Daniel down to Westbourne for the day. Well, as you can imagine, we jumped at the chance, and after a great morning racing about the beach, with Daniel barking at the waves, we were all ready for something to eat.

We left the car where it was in the car park by the beach and walked up the High Street to look for one of those nice fish and chip places where you get a big pot of tea and lots of bread and butter all included in the price. Angela wanted to go to the Princess Restaurant, but it looked far too posh and expensive, and after a lot of argument she had to give in.

She stopped sulking when we finally found a table in a cosy little café, especially when the big plates of food arrived. And if you've never eaten hot fish and chips and tomato ketchup and bread and butter at the seaside when the seabreeze has given you the appetite of an elephant you've never lived.

An elderly couple at the next table looked in horror at our mountains of food, and when the waitress came to take their order they asked if they could have small portions.

"We haven't got very big appetites, I'm afraid," said the old lady guiltily, as if it was something to be ashamed of.

"Oh, yer, that's OK," said the waitress cheerfully. "You can have children's portions if you like, half-price."

We were just scraping our plates when the elderly couple's order came. Two small portions of fish and chips, two cans of coke with straws, and two of the biggest orange ice-lollies you've ever seen.

"We didn't order these," stammered the old lady. "We don't want cokes and ice-lollies. Can't we have a pot of tea?"

"Nah," said the waitress. "Not with children's portions, you can't. Them's the rules. Sorry." And she plonked down the tray and hurried off to serve somebody else.

The elderly gentleman smiled at his wife.

"We'll drink coke for a change, dear," he said. "It might do us good. And I know somebody who won't mind taking these ice-lollies off our hands." And he leaned over and presented me and Angela with one each.

"Coo, that was a lucky bonus," said Angela, as we came out onto the pavement. My dad untied Daniel from the railing where we had left him with a handful of Boney Treats, and we all set off back to the car, with Angela and me happily licking our lollies. Half an hour later we weren't feeling quite so pleased with ourselves.

"Of course it was this car park," said my dad, tugging worriedly at what was left of his hair, after we had been all round the car park a couple of dozen times. "I remember the red and blue ticket-machine and everything."

Angela looked at him as if he was something that had escaped from a cage.

"Uncle Ted," she said patiently. "All the car parks in Westbourne probably have red and blue ticket-machines. The car isn't here, is it? So it must be somewhere else."

But it wasn't somewhere else. It was nowhere to be found. Even after we'd trudged round every car park in the whole town we couldn't find it, and finally we had to admit to ourselves that it had been stolen. That's when Angela had her fit of giggles, and she was still giggling when we all trooped into the Police Station to report the theft.

"We don't take stray dogs at this branch," said the sergeant on duty at the desk as we led Daniel in on his lead. "Take him straight to the Dog Rescue, please. Cranberry Drive."

"But I . . ." stuttered my dad helplessly. "It's not . . ."

The policeman leaned over the counter and put his face close to my dad's and you could see bits of breakfast bacon stuck in his teeth.

"NO DOGS!" he repeated more firmly, and it took ages to get through to him that it was a stolen car we wanted to report and that we hadn't brought Daniel in as a stray. But at last he got the message.

"What?" he said, looking suddenly very important and puffing out his chest. "Stolen car? Why didn't you say so in the first place?" And he pulled a form out of a drawer and began filling it in.

Angela stopped giggling when she discovered that my dad wasn't prepared to pay for a taxi home and that we all had to get the cold draughty train back to Edgebourne.

"Your dad's mean as well as stupid," she muttered crossly in my ear as we waited at the railway station, so I trod on her foot very hard which made her squeal like a baby pig but which made me feel a whole lot better.

We got home safely in the end, and my mum was all upset and cross about the car because it turned out it wasn't insured against theft and we didn't have any money for another one, not even second-hand.

"We'll just have to save up," said my dad with a sigh. "Travelling on the bus never hurt anybody, I suppose."

So we managed without a car for three whole days, until the Sunday morning when my dad was working in the garden and my mum was dozing upstairs with one of her headaches and the telephone rang.

"Who?" I said into the receiver. "West-bourne Police? You've found our car? Oh, great! Hang on, I'll get my dad."

My dad came rushing to the phone in his wellies, dropping great lumps of mud on the carpet in his hurry. But even my mum forgot to be cross when she heard the news.

Our car had been found by a farmer, in a tiny country lane about three miles out of Westbourne, and it seemed to be quite undamaged. Kids must have taken it for a joy-ride, the police reckoned, and had probably abandoned it there when they ran out of petrol.

"I've got a description of exactly where to find it," said my dad jubilantly. "The police suggest I go and pick it up straight away before vandals start removing the wheels and things. Come on, Charlie. Let's see if Angela's dad is busy. He might like to give us a lift down there."

Uncle Jim was pleased the car had been found, and didn't mind driving us down to Westbourne to get it back. Angela had to come too, of course, and Daniel as well, so after a quick snack lunch to keep us going we all piled into Uncle Jim's smart white Volvo. Soon we were belting down the motorway with Uncle Jim showing off how fast he could go and my dad keeping his hands over his eyes and trying not to look at the speedometer.

"This looks like the right track," said my dad, reading the map in the front seat, and we turned down a bumpy lane that only led to a farm.

"There it is!" shouted Angela excitedly in my ear, and sure enough, there was our dear old car, sitting quietly all by itself on the grass verge, and looking all forlorn and abandoned. Uncle Jim stopped the Volvo and we all got out and stood around the Morris and beamed at it as if it was a brand-new Rolls Royce. Even Daniel looked pleased, and cocked his leg against the front wheel to claim his property.

"I bet you've forgotten the keys, Uncle Ted," said Angela, with a cheeky grin, and my dad clapped his hand to his forehead in horror.

"It's all right, Dad," I said quickly, putting my tongue out at Angela. "Mum gave me her spare set." And I fished them out of my pocket and handed them over.

After putting a gallon of petrol into the tank from a spare can in his car, Uncle Jim drove off and left us to it.

"You don't mind, do you, Ted?" he said. "I've got a tennis match at three o'clock."

"That's all right, Jim," grinned my dad. "We'll be fine now. Thanks for the lift."

We watched the Volvo turn neatly in the narrow lane, and then zoom off back to the main road. Then we all got into the Morris, with me and Daniel in the back seat and Angela in the front as usual.

My dad sang silly songs as we set off for home, pleased that the car was none the worse for its adventure. But we had been on the main road for only five minutes when the singing suddenly stopped. He started saying rude words instead, for all at once a police patrol car appeared from nowhere, overtook us, and waved us down into the side of the road.

My dad turned red and looked as guilty as anything for no reason at all as the two policemen got out of their patrol car and strolled back along the road towards us. They walked all around our car, staring at the registration number and comparing it with a list one of them had in his hand. My dad couldn't stand the suspense. He opened the door and got out.

"Is everything all right, officer?" he said. "This is my car, you know."

The policemen were very polite, but they made it obvious that they just didn't believe him.

"It's down here as a stolen vehicle, sir," said the plump one with the weetabix-coloured moustache. "Our instructions are to bring in for questioning anyone found driving it. I'm afraid you'll have to come along with us. Unless you've got some proof of ownership, of course?"

My dad just stood there with his mouth hanging open, waiting for his voice to come back. When it did, he explained about the phone call and everything, but it all sounded a bit suspicious, especially as he'd rushed out without his wallet, where he kept all the car certificates and things.

"I suppose we could call up the Station," said weetabix-moustache doubtfully, and that's when Angela decided to play one of her horrible tricks.

Everybody turned to stare at her, because she had suddenly started to howl in the front seat. "Please don't arrest me," she sobbed through the open window. "It was nothing to do with me, honest. I'll die if you put me in a cell! Oh, Uncle Ted! Why did you do it?"

Honestly, I could have killed her. There was no chance the policemen would believe my dad's story now. They looked at one another and shook their heads.

"We can sort all this out at the Station, sir," said the thin one with the long red nose. "Perhaps you'd just follow us into Westbourne? It'll only take a few minutes to verify your story, I'm sure."

So there was nothing we could do but follow the patrol car to the Police Station, and when we arrived the two patrolmen ushered us towards the desk in front of them. I had brought Daniel in with me on his lead, and the sergeant at the desk leaped up when he saw him.

"No stray dogs at this branch," he said curtly. "Take him straight to the Dog Rescue, please. Cranberry Drive." Then he stared at us all, a baffled look growing on his face. "I've seen you lot before," he said suspiciously. "What's going on here?"

Everybody began talking at once and the

duty-sergeant had to bang on the desk for silence.

"ONE AT A TIME, PLEASE!" he bellowed, and was kind enough to let my dad tell his story first.

And so it all got gradually sorted out. And the two patrolmen didn't half look sheepish when they found out the car was really my dad's. But of course they were only doing their job, and it wasn't their fault if the farmer had only phoned the Police Station that morning and nobody had yet had time to let the patrol cars know. So they finally apologised and let us go, and we drove back up the motorway to Edgebourne, my dad quiet but relieved.

As for that stupid Angela, she sniggered and giggled all the way home. I hunched myself in the corner of the back seat and glowered at the back of her head. One of these days it'll be her that gets arrested, I promised myself darkly. But it wasn't Angela who got arrested next, after all. You'll never believe this, but it was Daniel.

Chapter Seven

DANIEL was arrested at the school Summer Fair in June, and I swore I would never forgive Angela as long as I lived because it was all her fault.

If only Miss Sopwith hadn't decided to have a cookery competition for the children in our class, none of it would have happened, so she's partly to blame as well, I suppose. She's dead keen on daft projects like that, and when she announced it one morning a couple of weeks before the Fair, everybody moaned and groaned like mad.

"You mean just the girls, though, Miss," called out Laurence Parker. "You don't really expect us lads to cook cakes and stuff, do you?"

Everybody sniggered and Laurence's round moon face went as red as a London bus when Miss Sopwith insisted that even the boys had to take part.

"It never did a boy any harm to learn to cook, Laurence," she said. "And girls should learn woodwork, too, for that matter. I shall ask Miss Collingwood to sample your efforts, and of course there'll be a prize for the nicest cakes or pastries."

"What's the prize, Miss? A needlework box?" said Laurence with a cheeky grin, and everybody sniggered some more. Then Miss Sopwith gave us one of her watch-it-or-you'll-all-be-kept-in-after-school looks and we all decided we'd better shut up.

There was one person who didn't moan a bit, however. It was that Delilah Jones. And of course she was smirking all over her silly face because her dad's a Master Chef in a big posh hotel and she's been baking cakes since she was in her cot or maybe even sooner. Everybody knew from the start who was bound to win the competition, so there wasn't much point in having it at all.

Angela, who can't stand anyone to be better than her, was silent and thoughtful on the way home. I knew better than to pester her when I could see she was working out one of her plots, so I just kept quiet and let her think. It wasn't until that evening after tea that she charged in through our back door and came dancing upstairs into my bedroom with such a huge smile on her face I thought she'd won the pools.

"I've got it, Charlie," she said triumphantly, and I stared at her gloomily. After that dancing display I was dead suspicious of anything she suggested and I didn't want to know about any more of her horrible tricks.

"What have you got?" I said. "Measles? Chicken-pox? If so you can just get out of here before you give it to me."

Angela giggled and flung herself on my bed. "Sabotage!" she said, bouncing about like a three-year-old. "That's how we'll fix Delilah

Jones. We'll put something really nasty in her cake when nobody's looking, and let somebody else win old Soppy's cookery prize. Me, for example," she added with a grin. "Or possibly even you, Charlie Ellis. Although if you produce anything like those biscuits you made for the Senior Citizens' tea party, it won't only be them that need false teeth!"

I grabbed a pillow and bashed her over the head with it and of course she grabbed the other one and bashed me back and in no time at all we were rolling about, thumping each other as hard as we could and making the bed bounce so much it almost went through the window. Then Daniel came bursting in to see what all the noise was about and as soon as he saw what was going on he decided at once that this was his sort of game. He launched himself onto the bed between us and began to yelp and growl and worry the pillows with his sharp teeth which really made the feathers fly. And soon we were screaming with laughter at his antics as he rushed about chasing feathers as if they were live ducks, and it must have sounded like bedlam because my dad suddenly appeared in the doorway with a not-very-pleased expression on his face.

"Oo-er!" said Angela, and hastily scrambled off the bed. I got off too and we both stood there sheepishly with feathers in our hair and in our ears and all over our clothes.

Dear old Daniel saved the day. A large feather came floating down from the ceiling, and with a quick pounce he caught it in his mouth and presented it proudly to my dad. And of course it was impossible for my dad to stay annoyed after that and all three of us ended up giggling together like three little kids.

"We'd better get this mess cleared up before your mum sees it," was all my dad said, and he even gave us a hand.

I don't know why but after he'd gone I suddenly found I wasn't cross with Angela any more, and I even listened when she told me her plan for fixing that show-off Delilah Jones.

"She's sure to do some sort of really fancy gateau," Angela said. "You know, all filled with fresh cream and stuff. What I thought was, while Shirley What'sname from *Westenders* is cutting the ribbon and declaring the Fair open, you and I could get some of your dad's shaving foam and ..."

"Hang on," I interrupted with a scowl. "My dad's shaving foam? Why my dad's shaving foam? Why not your dad's shaving foam, Angela Mitchell?"

She looked at me as if I was a total idiot. "Because my dad uses an electric razor, stupid," she said. "He doesn't use shaving foam, does he? All right?"

"Right," I said meekly, liking the idea less and less when I saw that it was me that was getting the worst part to play. Then another sudden thought made my stomach churn like a tank full of tadpoles.

"Have you forgotten who's judging the competition, Angela?" I said fearfully. "I don't like to think about Miss Collingwood getting a mouthful of shaving cream!" And I shuddered in horror at the thought.

"Oh, she'll only spit it out," said Angela airily. "It's not exactly poison, is it? It's not exactly *deadly nightshade*." And she went off into a fit of helpless giggles at the expression on my face, because once she'd pretended to poison Laurence Parker with deadly nightshade, and I had been stupid enough to believe her.

In the end I agreed to her plan, provided that all I had to do was get the shaving foam and she would put it in the cake herself. That way it would be her that got into trouble if we were caught, and nobody need know about my part in the plot. Unless she told them, that is, and she's quite capable of that.

Angela didn't say another word about it for almost two weeks, and I began to hope she'd changed her mind about the whole thing. But she turned up in our kitchen on the Friday evening before the Fair, and she laughed like a baboon when she saw me because I was swathed from head to foot in my mum's biggest apron, with smudges of flour on my nose and cheeks.

I wasn't pleased to see her, as you can imagine. I had been really enjoying myself mixing my chocolate cake with a great big wooden spoon and having a lick every so often to make sure it tasted all right. My mum had helped me choose an easy recipe from one of her cookery books, and had shown me how to set the oven properly and things like that, so I really thought I had a chance of winning the prize.

"What's up?" I said grumpily, beating the mixture even harder and wishing it was Angela's brains in the bowl. "Why aren't you at home baking your cake for the competition?"

She scooped up a bit of the mixture on her finger, tasted it, and made a face as if she'd swallowed a mouthful of mud. "Yuck!" she said. "Charlie, that's the most disgusting stuff I've ever tasted. It's like brown sick!"

I scowled. "How do you know?" I retorted. "When have you ever tasted brown sick?" And she went off into one of those peals of girlish laughter that I've seen her practising in front of the mirror.

"Anyway," she said, when she'd recovered. "I'm not making a cake at all. Mum's been to London today, and she brought me half-a-dozen of those yummy chocolate éclairs from Fortnums. So that's saved me the bother."

I almost hit her on the head with the wooden spoon. "Angela!" I said, horrified. "That's cheating! I'm really surprised at your mum!"

"Oh, I didn't tell her they were for a competition, you clot," said Angela. "I just said we had to take something for the cake stall, that's all. Anyway, who's to know? You wouldn't tell on me, Charlie, would you?"

I shook my head hurriedly, knowing full well I wouldn't dare. In any case I don't believe in telling tales on your friends, no matter what they've done. It might be soppy of me, but that's the way I am, and that's how Angela can get away with murder so often.

"Anyway, Charlie," she said. "I didn't come round to tell you about that. I came round for the shaving foam. Have you got it yet?"

My legs felt all wobbly and my throat went dry. "Er, no," I said. "I haven't had a chance yet. In any case I'll have to leave it until my dad's had his shave in the morning, won't I? Otherwise he'll ask where it's gone, won't he?"

Even Angela could see the sense of this, so she had to be satisfied with my promise that I'd bring the stuff to the Fair the next day. As soon as I heard her slam the back door on her way out I breathed a sigh of relief and got back to work on my cake. And it turned out really lovely, especially when I put chocolate butter cream in the middle and chocolate icing on the top and decorated it with chocolate buttons and walnuts. My mum and dad both came in to see it when they'd finished watching 'One Man And His Dog' on the telly, and they both said it looked yummy. My dad even scraped the bowl, much to my mum's disgust.

"You've just consumed about two hundred calories," she complained. "What about your diet? You should have had an apple instead. An apple's only thirty-five."

"Thirty-six if there's a maggot in it," said my dad, wiping chocolate off his chin, and my mum shuddered and went back to the telly.

The next morning dawned bright and sunny, and I lay in bed for a while wondering why I felt so squiggly in my stomach. Then I heard my dad singing, "Figaro here, Figaro there, Figaro everywhere", which he always sings when he's shaving, and I pulled the covers over my head and wished I didn't have to get up at all.

But Angela would be furious if I let her down, so I listened until I heard my dad go along the landing to his bedroom, then I slipped quickly out of bed, dashed into the bathroom and grabbed the can of shaving foam from the shelf. I was just about to run out of the bathroom with it when my dad suddenly appeared in the doorway. I shoved the can quickly behind my back but it was too late. He'd already seen it. And I don't think I've ever seen him look so astonished in his life.

"What on earth are you doing, Charlie?" he said. "You're a bit young to be starting shaving, aren't you?"

I felt my face go as pink as the bathroom wallpaper. I gazed at the carpet for a long time, wondering what to say. I hate telling fibs, especially to my dad, so there was only one thing to do.

"It was for a joke," I explained lamely. "But it doesn't matter. I've changed my mind." I shoved the shaving foam into his hand and escaped as fast as I could, leaving him standing there scratching his bald patch with a baffled expression on his face.

The Fair was to be opened at ten o'clock, so at nine-thirty my mum wrapped my cake carefully in greaseproof paper, popped it in the boot of the car, and we all set off for the school field, including Daniel, who had been brushed until his coat shone like satin, ready for the dog show in the afternoon.

We drove through the village of Edgebourne with me racking my brains for an excuse to give Angela, and just as we were passing the baker's shop my mum touched my dad's arm.

"Stop here for a second, Ted, will you?" she said. "I just want to pop in here for some fresh bread."

"There's something I have to get, too," I mumbled, and as soon as the car stopped I shot out of the back seat and round the corner to the chemist's. I spent the last of my pocket money on a big can of shaving foam, and made sure the assistant wrapped it up so nobody could see what it was. I dashed back to the car with a big bulge up my T-shirt, and if my dad noticed he didn't say a word. I fell back against the cushions, grateful that at least I wouldn't have Angela furious with me. She's like an octopus with sore feet when she doesn't get her own way.

Anyway, she was already at the cake exhibition when I got there, arranging her Fort-num's chocolate éclairs on one of the plates Miss Sopwith had provided, and propping her name-card in front.

"Hi, Charlie," she called. "Isn't it a lovely day. The weather forecast said it's going to be twenty-five degrees Centipede."

"Centigrade," I said, unwrapping my cake and putting it next to Angela's. "You mean twenty-five degrees Centigrade."

Angela looked at me as if I had egg on my chin.

"That's what I said, stupid," she replied care-lessly, and I knew there was no point in arguing. I shoved the can of shaving foam into her hands, glad to get rid of it at last, and turned to rush off after my mum and dad, who were joining the crowd at the gate to see the Fair opened.

"Oy! Where d'you think you're going?" said Angela, pulling me back towards her. "You don't think I'm going to do this all by myself, do you? The least you could do is keep an eye open in case anybody's coming."

I hadn't bargained for this, but there didn't seem any way I could get out of it.

"Hurry up, then," I muttered hastily. "I can see Shirley What'sname cutting the ribbon now."

So while everybody was looking at the pretty young actress, in her slinky pink dress and flowery hat, Angela went along the row of cakes until she found Delilah Jones's name-card. And sure enough, the cake was a great big creamy gateau, all decorated with cherries and grated chocolate. It looked so delicious it seemed a shame to spoil it, but that didn't bother Angela. She carefully lifted off the top half and scraped all the whipped cream out of the middle with the cake-knife she found on the table. She looked round for somewhere to dump the cream, and her eyes lit up when she realised I had Daniel beside me on his lead.

"Here you are, Daniel," she said. "A lovely treat for you."

It was no use my protesting that all that rich cream would make him sick, because Daniel loves cream better than anything in the world and had scoffed the lot before I could say a word. He was even jumping up at the table for more, and I had to drag him away while Angela quickly re-filled the gateau with a thick layer of shaving foam. When she put the top back on the cake, she squirted more foam round the sides so you couldn't see it had been tampered with, then to my horror and disgust she gave me back the empty can.

"Chuck it in the bin when you get a chance," she said, and I hurriedly shoved it back up my T-shirt. I was only just in time. The crowd at the gate broke up just then and people began to wander about the field, trying their luck at the coconut shies and tombola and 'guess how many buttons in the jar' and things like that. And Miss Sopwith suddenly appeared and cooed in delight when she saw all the beautiful cakes and apple pies and jam tarts.

I decided to make myself scarce, but I had a heck of a job dragging Daniel away now that he'd had a taste of that yummy cream.

"I see your dog is a cake-lover, Charlie," smiled Miss Sopwith, busy cutting a slice from each one for Miss Collingwood to taste.

"He'd scoff the lot if he got the chance," I admitted, and finally managed to haul him away. He hadn't forgotten where they were, though, because Angela and I were just coming away from the hoop-la stall with a big cuddly rabbit that Angela had won, when Daniel suddenly wriggled out of his collar and raced away across the field. "Quick, Angela!" I gasped. "He's after the cakes again!" And we both set off in pursuit.

We managed to catch up with him all right. *Just too late to stop him from gobbling up the slice that Miss Sopwith had cut from Delilah Jones's gateau.* Luckily nobody had noticed him pinching it, so I grabbed him and carried him away. But he wriggled so hard I had to drop him and all of a sudden he started to race round in circles and howl and shake his head and altogether behave in a most peculiar way.

It was then I could have murdered Angela because she suddenly began to scream at the top of her voice and point at Daniel and shout, "Help!" and "Mad dog!" and "Rabies!" and daft things like that. Then Daniel fell over on his back and waved his feet in the air as white froth poured out of his mouth and spattered the grass around him.

In no time at all the whole field took up the cry. "Rabid dog! Phone the police!" everybody shouted, and there was a stampede towards the gate away from the poor animal, who was still writhing on the ground frantically pawing his face to get rid of the horrible taste.

I knelt down beside him and tried to clean him up with my hanky but the foam kept on coming out of his mouth, and I was just getting in a panic when my dad suddenly arrived on the scene. His eyes almost fell out of his head like golfballs when he saw the state poor Daniel was in, and without listening to a word I was trying to tell him he dragged me away to safety. And somebody must have phoned the police because a police van suddenly roared into the field with its siren blaring. It stopped beside Daniel and two uniformed policemen wearing thick padded gauntlets got out and they grabbed my poor dog, shoved him into the back of the van and drove rapidly away. The last I saw of Daniel was his little bewildered face peering out through the bars of the window at the back.

Angela burst out laughing and I burst into tears and flung myself at my dad's chest and he stroked my hair and said, "There, there, bonny lass," until I managed to calm down.

At last, through lots of sobs and hiccups and nose-blowing, I blurted out what had happened, and my good old dad wasted no time. He bundled me into the car and raced off to the police station to the rescue. When we got there Daniel had already been examined by a police vet and given a clean bill of health. He was sitting dolefully in a cage looking like the most miserable dog in the world, and as soon as I told the vet the story he let him out at once. And I don't know who was the happiest, Daniel or me.

In the end, the day wasn't as disastrous as I'd thought, because when we got back to the Fair I found that the cakes had been judged and I'd actually won first prize. It was a beautiful book called 'The Birds of Britain', all full of lovely pictures of kingfishers and goldfinches and things. And of course Angela was so livid she almost choked, especially when I gave the book to Delilah Jones. I don't know who was the more astonished, but I knew it was the right thing to do.

Then in the afternoon Angela was even more livid, because believe it or not Daniel walked off with first prize in the dog show. He won a beautiful silver cup, and I was so proud I almost burst, especially when the judge, Miss Judy Kayter, said she'd never seen a spaniel with such a lovely glossy coat.

I reckon it was probably all that cream that did it. I suggested that to my dad on the way home and he laughed.

"Or maybe it was all that shaving foam!" he said. And Daniel barked and grinned, just as if he knew exactly what we were saying.

THIS WEEK
ONLY
Have your ears pierced
quickly and painlessly.
only £2·50

No intment
r ired

Chapter Eight

THREE new children came into our class that term, two girls and a boy. And they are all very nice, especially the boy, who's called Dwight Johnson. He's so good-looking and such good fun that Angela has made up her mind to marry him when she grows up.

"I bet he hasn't even asked you," I said when she told me, but she only tossed her head and said that if he didn't ask her she would ask him.

I said he would probably ask one of the new

girls, Jessica Brown or Amanda Barrett. Jessica is sweet and quiet and pretty with shiny dark hair, and Amanda is not only pretty but she wears earrings in school.

That caused a right hoo-ha with Miss Sopwith when she saw them, I can tell you, and she told Amanda to take them out at once. But Amanda had brought a note from her mother to say that she'd just had her ears pierced, and she had to wear these tiny earrings called 'sleepers' to stop the holes from healing up again.

Miss Sopwith wasn't very pleased, but there wasn't a lot she could do about it. And so that's what started Angela on about getting her ears done, too. There's nothing she hates more than somebody having something she hasn't got, and she brooded about it for weeks.

One day near the end of term Angela and Jessica Brown and I were on our way home from school together, and we were just passing that posh new *Style Hairdressers* when Angela grabbed our arms and pulled us round to face the window. 'Special offer', said a big notice stuck on the glass. 'This week only. Have your ears pierced, quickly and painlessly. Only £2.50. No appointment required'.

Jessica shuddered and went as pale as paper. "No thanks," she said quickly. "I can't even stand injections. It would kill me to get my ears pierced." And she shook herself free and ran off home by herself.

Somehow I seem to be the only one stupid enough to get trapped into Angela's schemes. I don't know how she does it, because my dad says I'm twice as bright as she is, but she seems to get me involved before I know what's happening. And in no time at all, standing there outside the hairdressers, she had me thinking it would be really great to have pierced ears, and wear earrings like Amanda Barrett, even though I detest needles and run a mile if I even see a wasp.

Angela was hopping up and down with excitement at the idea, especially when she remembered it would be the end of term party soon, and that this year Miss Sopwith was organising a country dance, with a band and a supper and everything.

"Just think, Charlie," said Angela. "All the

boys will want us to be their partners for the dancing. Even that dishy Dwight Johnson!"

I think that's probably what convinced me in the end, because although I hadn't said a word about it to Angela, I quite fancy Dwight Johnson myself. And I'm sure he likes me better than her, because he said he'd help me with my limerick for Miss Sopwith's latest competition.

She's crazy about competitions, our Miss Sopwith is, and this time she'd come up with the bright idea of a limerick contest. We were all supposed to stand up and recite them at the end-of-term dance, and the winner would be the one who made the audience laugh and clap the most.

I was nearly going mad, because I had thought up a brilliant limerick last year when we were on holiday, but I still hadn't managed to get past the first two lines.

There was a young vampire called Dracula
Whose habits were really spectacular ...

And there I was stuck. Even my dad couldn't think of an ending, and I was beginning to think

I would have to write a new one altogether before the thing drove me round the bend. Then I had the idea of asking Dwight Johnson. It's just the sort of thing he's good at, and when he said he'd give it some thought I felt quite hopeful at last.

But days went by and he never mentioned it again. I began to think he just couldn't be bothered, and I didn't want to pester him. Have you noticed that boys hate being pestered by girls, especially when there are other boys around? It's funny that, because girls never seem to mind being pestered by boys.

Anyway, when Angela came up with her ear-piercing idea I couldn't help feeling tempted. Maybe I thought it would make Dwight take more notice of me or something. So we dashed off home after seeing the advert in the hair-dresser's window, and we found both our mums together in my mum's kitchen, drinking tea and scoffing naughty vanilla slices without leaving any for us.

"You can have a biscuit, if you like," said my mum when we complained. "You don't want to spoil your dinner, do you."

I don't know how cream cakes in the afternoon never spoil grown-ups' dinners, while children are never allowed more than one measly plain digestive. Even Daniel was better off than me. He got the cake box to lick out. When I grow up I'm going to have six children, and give them as many cream cakes as they want every day.

Angela nudged my arm as we sat down at the table with our biscuits, and I looked at her in alarm.

"Go on, ask," she hissed behind her hand. "You know, earrings!"

I hadn't realised it was going to be me that had to ask, but I took a deep breath and gabbled out about the special offer. And I don't know why I thought we would get permission but of course we didn't. At the very mention of the words 'ears pierced', Auntie Sally let out a loud shriek and jumped up from the table.

"You're coming home with me at once, my girl," she told Angela firmly, ignoring her pleas. "And we'll have no more of this silly talk. You're far too young to wear earrings. I suppose it was Charlie's idea. You'll be wanting to wear make-up next!" And she dragged the protesting Angela round the corner to her own house.

I knew better than to try to persuade my mum after she had said no. Even when I reminded her that my cousin Fiona had her ears pierced when she was only three, she still wouldn't hear of it. She was very nice about it, though, and promised that in a couple of years' time when I was a bit older she'd let me get them done. So I had to be content with that.

I spent the evening after dinner in my room working on my limerick, and after racking my brains for about two hours I decided to give up Dracula and start something new. And this is what I finally came up with.

A careless young gardener called Joe,
Accidentally mowed off his toe.
The family beagle
Swiftly and eagerl-
Y swallowed it down in one go.

I showed it to my mum and she groaned. "It's awful, Charlie," she said. And I couldn't help but agree.

I didn't throw the limerick away though. I gave it to Angela when she came begging for me to help her with hers. She can't write a limerick to save her life, and she was so grateful she promised to buy me a present on Saturday when she got her pocket money. I said it was a lousy limerick and I didn't want a present, but she'd made up her mind and there's no arguing with her.

So when Saturday came she turned up on the doorstep all dressed up to go for a walk round Edgebourne. I would much rather have stayed at home and played with Daniel in the garden but she wouldn't take no for an answer. And even though I knew by the greenish colour of her eyes that she was plotting something, I found myself putting on my coat and going with her.

"Bring Daniel with you," she said. "The walk will do him good."

Well, I couldn't understand that at all. She normally can't be bothered with dogs and thinks Daniel is the stupidest dog she's ever seen, but Daniel was jumping up and down hopefully and I hadn't the heart to leave him behind.

We strolled into the village and as soon as we were in the High Street I realised what she was up to because she dragged me straight over to *Style Hairdressers*. And you should have seen how my mouth opened and shut in astonishment when she pulled a five pound note out of her pocket and waved it in front of my nose.

"Dare you, Charlie?" she said, her eyes glinting all green and evil like a witch's. "I'll dare if you will. I'll even go first if you like."

I tried to argue but she wouldn't listen. She said that once it was done there was nothing anybody could do about it. She said there'd be a row at first, but it would blow over in a few days.

"That's how Amanda Barrett got hers done," she told me. "If she can do it I don't see why we can't."

"Come on, then," I said hastily before I changed my mind. "We'll go in together, and you can be first." But Angela was shaking her head.

"We can't both go in," she said. "One of us will have to wait outside with Daniel. They won't let him in there." She opened the door of the hairdressers and walked jauntily in. "I won't be long, Charlie," she said over her shoulder. "Wish me luck."

I stood outside and waited for a minute or two, and my knees were knocking so much they were like castanets in a band. And the longer I waited the more scared I got, and then I thought of my mum's face when she found out and how disappointed in me my dad would be and how upset they would both be that I could disobey them like that. Finally my nerve failed me altogether and I was just beginning to slink away round the corner when the door opened and Angela came out.

"Where are you sneaking off to, Charlie?" she said in a shocked voice. "I don't believe you're chickening out now, when I've been and had mine done!"

I looked at her and she had two tiny bits of sticking plaster stuck on the lobes of her ears.

"Er, no," I lied. "Of course not. Did it hurt?"

"Not a bit," she said gleefully. "Just a tiny prick, that's all," She handed me two pound coins and a fifty pence piece. "Go on, Charlie.

Your turn now." And she took Daniel's lead from my hand and pushed me through the door.

I stood on the soft plushy carpet beside the reception desk and sniffed the smelly perm smells and the hair sprays and listened to the soothing music and watched a lady with a big nose having her hair dyed purple. Then a girl with bright orange hair sticking straight up from her head as if she had seen a ghost came along and looked me up and down.

"Yes?" she said, with a smile that showed all her gold fillings, and I knew there was nothing I could do now except take the plunge.

"I'd like to have my ears pierced," I squeaked in a tiny voice.

"Pardon?" said the girl. "What did you say?"

So I cleared my throat and said it again and this time it came out in a big loud croak that made everybody turn round and stare which didn't make me feel any better, I can tell you.

But the orange-haired girl didn't think there was anything strange in my request. She led me straight to a seat in front of a long row of mirrors and put a towel round my shoulders.

"That's to catch the blood," she joked, trying to cheer me up. But it didn't cheer me up in the least. It made my knees knock even more. I tried to grin back at her but my teeth were stuck together with superglue. I looked in the mirror and my eyes looked huge and scared in my pastry-coloured face.

I suddenly realised that the girl was holding out a small tray for me to look at.

"Which earrings would you like?" she was saying, and I pulled myself together and looked at the little gold hearts and pearl drops and sparkly bits of diamond. In the end I chose the hearts, partly because I liked the idea of hearts, but mainly because they were the smallest and would show the least.

I watched fearfully while the girl fitted one of the hearts into a thing that looked a bit like the staple-gun my dad borrows sometimes from the office. Then she drew little ink-spots on the lobes of my ears and asked me if I thought they were in the right place.

I hadn't a clue whether they were in the right place or not but I said yes just to get it over with more quickly. The girl dabbed some stuff on my ears that made them feel cold, then she pressed the gun against my right ear-lobe.

"Ready?" she said, smiling encouragingly at me in the mirror. "This might sting a bit, but only for a second or two."

I nodded that I was ready and shut my eyes tight. There was a sudden bang right in my ear and a shooting pain that almost made me fall off the chair.

"Ouch!" I said, blinking back the tears, and the girl laughed.

"Makes your eyes water, dunnit?" she sniggered. "Bet you don't want the other one done now, do you?"

I didn't. But I wasn't going to let her know that. So I gritted my teeth and closed my eyes again.

"I'm ready," I said.

There was another bang and another stinging pain even worse than the first. Then it was all over and she was taking the towel off my shoulders and helping me off the chair.

"Bathe them every day with surgical spirit," she told me. "Leave the earrings in all the time for six weeks. And keep twiddling them around in the holes to keep them nice and open." She gave me a grin. "Otherwise they'll heal up," she said, "and you'll have to come and get them done again. And you wouldn't like that, would you?"

I said I wouldn't, and paid over the two pounds fifty Angela had given me.

"What about the sticking plaster?" I asked suddenly, on my way to the door. The girl looked totally blank. "Sticking plaster?" she said. "Oh, you mustn't cover them up. You have to keep the holes open, like I told you."

I went outside to find Angela, my poor ears burning like sausages on a barbecue, and I knew as soon as I saw her that once again I'd been had. She was sitting on the library steps, carefully peeling off the bits of sticking-plaster from her ears and throwing them into the gutter. *And there wasn't a single earring in sight.*

She fell down the steps laughing when I appeared with my little gold hearts.

"Ooh, Charlie!" she said. "You've really gone and done it now! You won't half catch it when you get home!"

I stared at her as if she was one of those bags

of manure that Mr Willick puts on his potato patch.

"You're rotten and horrible and I hate you," I managed to blurt out. "I never want to be your friend again." And I grabbed Daniel's lead from her and rushed off home.

Angela looked very upset. She followed me all the way, explaining that it was only a joke, and all she had done in the hairdressers was get the fiver changed and borrow their loo so that she could fix the bits of sticking-plaster on her ears. She said she was very sorry and she even promised that she'd get hers done the next day.

But I took no notice. I went straight home and upstairs to my room and put my pillow over my head to stop my ears from throbbing and I howled and howled until I must have fallen asleep. And that's where my mum found me when she came to call me for lunch.

"Charlie! What on earth's the matter?" she said, when she saw my red eyes and blotchy face.

I didn't say anything. All I did was push my hair back away from my ears to show the tell-tale gold hearts. And after staring at me speechlessly for a whole minute my mum marched grimly out of my room and slammed the door, which made me howl all over again.

After a while I heard my dad's car in the drive. Then came the sound of their voices arguing. Then I heard feet on the stairs and knew they were coming to attack me together so I dived out of bed and crawled under it.

"She was here a few minutes ago," I heard my mum say in a puzzled voice, and I stared at her pink furry slippers and at my dad's white tennis shoes until a bit of fluff got up my nose and I sneezed.

So my dad bent down and hauled me out and sat me on the bed, and they sat down one on each side of me so I couldn't escape and I was just about to start howling again to make them feel sorry for me when, to my utter astonishment, I realised they were both smiling.

I looked from one to the other, and my mum took hold of my hand.

"Your dad doesn't think it's such a crime to want to look pretty," she said, a bit sheepishly. "And he's just been reminding me of something. I did exactly the same thing myself when I was your age. So I've really no right at all to be cross."

My eyes almost filled up with tears again when she gave me a hug, and then she pulled a small velvet-covered box from her pocket. "These are my first earrings," she said. "They belonged to my grandmother. I'd like you to have them, Charlie."

And they both beamed all over their faces at my cries of joy when I opened the box and found the prettiest pair of earrings you ever saw. They were tiny loops of gold, with a real flame-coloured garnet set in each one, and I knew they would be perfect with my best party-dress which I planned to wear for the school dance.

I did wear them, too. And I was the belle of the ball. All the boys wanted to dance with me, especially that dishy Dwight Johnson. Angela was so mad she was almost sick, especially when Dwight kept whispering in my ear and making me giggle.

"What's he been saying to you, Charlie?" she demanded crossly, when we all sat down to hear the limerick competition. "It must have been very funny to make you laugh like that."

I wouldn't tell her, though. I just hugged the words to me like a hot-water bottle, all through the boring old limericks, until it was my turn. I stood up, a bit nervously, but Dwight grinned at me and gave me a thumbs-up sign. I felt better at once, and spoke up in a loud, clear voice.

There once was a vampire called Dracula,
Whose habits were truly spectacular.
Every dark night
He'd go for a BITE,
And scrape up the blood with a spatula!

As usual it was Laurence Parker who started the great guffaws of laughter, but this time I could have kissed him because he soon had the whole school roaring and cheering and stamping their feet and laughing so much Miss Sopwith could hardly get them to stop.

Angela gnashed her teeth when the result was announced and she heard I'd won the limerick contest. Especially when she saw the prize, a huge box of chocolate-coated candies from Harrods.

"You'll share them with me, won't you, Charlie," she said confidently, as we came out of school when the party was over. "I *am* your best friend."

But I didn't give her a single one. I'd had enough of her making a fool of me all the time and I wouldn't even walk home with her. Dwight and I walked home together, and we finished the whole box of candies, laughing at our silly limerick all the way.

Rabble Starkey by Lois Lowry

£2.99

Rabble's mother, Sweet Hosanna, had Rabble (whose real name is Parable) when she was only fourteen, and life's been one long struggle for both of them. Now they're faced with losing their home, with nowhere to go.

A Summer to Die by Lois Lowry

£2.99

Having a sister who is blonde and pretty and popular can be tricky if you're like Meg — serious, hardworking and, well, plain. But when Molly becomes critically ill, Meg has to face up to something much worse than jealousy.

Find a Stranger, Say Goodbye
by Lois Lowry

£2.99

Natalie has everything a girl could want: a lively and caring family, success at school, beauty, and yet, knowing she is adopted, she is obsessed by the idea of finding her natural mother and discovering why she gave up her baby girl.

Number the Stars by Lois Lowry
(Newbery Award Winner 1990)

£2.99

Copenhagen, 1943. Annemarie carries on her normal life under the shadow of the Nazis — until they begin their campaign to "relocate" the Jews of Denmark. Annemarie's best friend Ellen is a Jew, and Annemarie is called upon to help Ellen and many others escape across the sea.

Beyond the Rolling River by Kate Andrew
£2.75
Toby and his chameleon friend Hardly Visible are desperately trying to find Glimrod, the lost Tuning Fork which controls the weather. Most important of all, they have to find it before Slubblejum the Nethercat does — for whoever controls the weather rules the world!

The Prism Tree by Kate Andrew
£2.75
Toby and Hardly Visible are determined to foil Slubblejum's terrible plot to cut down the Prism Tree, for without the Tree there would be no colour in the world. But Toby and his friend are prisoners on the nethercat's ship. Can they escape in time?

Black Harvest by Ann Pilling
£2.75
The ruggest west coast of Ireland seems like the perfect place for a holiday. Then everything starts to go wrong. Prill's dreams are haunted by a starving woman; Baby Alison falls sick with a strange illness; Colin is aware of an awful smell. Only Oliver, their cousin remains unnervingly calm...

The Witch of Lagg by Ann Pilling
£2.25
The ancient castle of Lagg hides a secret, though it's nothing as straightforward as a vampire. It's something with a very strange power. As Colin, Prill and Oliver explore the rambling old house and the dark woods surrounding it, they find themselves becoming the victims of some evil force, something full of threat...

ORDER FORM

To order direct from the publishers, just make a list of the titles you want and fill in the form below:

Name_____

Address_____

_____

_____

Send to: Dept 6, HarperCollins Publishers Ltd, Westerhill Road, Bishopbriggs, Glasgow G64 2QT.

Please enclose a cheque or postal order to the value of the cover price, plus:

UK & BFPO: Add £1.00 for the first book, and 25p per copy for each addition book ordered.

Overseas and Eire: Add £2.95 service charge. Books will be sent by surface mail but quotes for airmail despatch will be given on request.

A 24-hour telephone ordering service is available to Visa and Access card holders:

041-772 2281